Poker Face

Poker Face

a girlhood among gamblers

Katy Lederer

crown publishers new york

Published by Crown Publishers, New York, New York.
Member of the Crown Publishing Group, a division of Random House, Inc.
www.randomhouse.com

CROWN is a trademark and the Crown colophon is a registered trademark of Random House, Inc.

Printed in the United States of America

Design by Barbara Sturman

Library of Congress Cataloging-in-Publication Data
Lederer, Katy.
Poker face : a girlhood among gamblers / Katy Lederer.
p. cm.
1. Lederer, Katy—Childhood and youth. 2. Lederer, Katy—Homes and haunts—Nevada—Las Vegas. 3. Poets, American—20th century—Biography. 4. Las Vegas (Nev.)—Social life and customs. 5. Gambling—Nevada—Las Vegas. 6. Gamblers—Nevada—Las Vegas. 7. Family—Nevada—Las Vegas. I. Title.
PS3612 .E3417 Z49 2003
811'.6—dc21
2002154357

ISBN 0-609-60898-3

10 9 8 7 6 5 4 3

First Edition

for my family

acknowledgments

Here let me offer the most inadequate thanks to the people who have been brought into these pages. Love and respect to my mother and father, who answered innumerable questions with both empathy and compassion; gratitude to my sister and brother for their patience and understanding; and thanks to all the poker players whose fascinating lives enriched my family's life.

Sarah Arvio, Cornelia Calder, Maggie Cassidy, Patricia Chui, Rachel Cohen, Ben Duke, Sophie Fels, Tim Hodge, Timothy Liu, Anna Moschovakis, Stefania Pandolfo, Claudia Rankine, Geoff Shandler, Matt Surman, Monica Youn, Steve Zolotow, Magdalena Zurawski, and many friends at Yaddo offered invaluable criticism and encouragement throughout the writing process; Tim Hodge, Howard and Susan Lederer, the Schlesinger Program at St. Paul's School, and the Corporation of Yaddo offered invaluable time. Special thanks are due to Rick Barot, Kevin Larimer, Vanessa Mobley, Natasha Schüll, and Prageeta Sharma for their critical generosity; to Susan Evans for her support; and to my father for listening to so many of these words over the telephone. Gratitude also to Peter McGuigan for his extraordinary devotion to this project, to Dorianne Steele for her wonderful help, and to Pete Fornatale, my unmatchable editor at Crown, for helping me to make this book the best it could be.

Though this is a work of nonfiction, some identifying characteristics and locations have been altered to protect the parties involved. And though this is truly a memoir in that the substance of the story emanates from memory rather than imagination, most of the dialogue has been fictionalized. Rather than fabricate details, I have done my best to fill in fragmentary recollections by drawing on related events, and in a very few chapters, such as "Old Money" and "Façades," I have combined several related recollections into a single, representative story.

Finally, and perhaps needless to say, many of my memories diverge in significant ways from those of other members of the family, and by rendering them as I do here, I mean neither to discredit nor deny their alternative versions.

contents

II

Pride is faith in the idea that God had, when he made us. A proud man is conscious of the idea, and aspires to realize it. He does not strive toward a happiness, or comfort, which may be irrelevant to God's idea of him. His success is the idea of God, successfully carried through, and he is in love with his destiny.

—Isak Dinesen
from "On Pride"

Nothing is more indicatible of civilizations than the solaces that people seek.

—Zelda Fitzgerald
from her notebooks

prologue

The Green Glasses

Inside the bag it was money. That was all. Hundreds in paper-banded bundles of $5,000. Back at home, it had been tens and twenties, but here in New York it was "C notes" and "Benjamins." A stack of ten was called "a dime," while only one was called "a dollar."

Before I looked inside the bag, which sagged open on the backseat of the cab, I supposed it was cocaine (clear white bags, like sugar), or possibly heroin. I think that's what I must have thought, though I can't remember now. What I do remember is taking a conscious mental picture of the contents of the bag, mindful of the fact that this was a grave, important moment—that all of this money was a glowing green portal between the tedious past and some glorious future. I was riding around in a new yellow cab, a pair of fancy glasses in my pocket, off to some destination I knew would be glamorous. "You've got to keep your mouth shut" was all that my brother had said. "He'll think it's pretty weird that I brought you along."

I'd arrived in New York from New Hampshire that morning. My father had dropped me at the local city bus terminal, handed me my two-way fare, and told me to give his regards to Annie and Howard, my sister and brother, who were, respectively, seven and nine years older than I. Both were in New York—Annie near Columbia, where she was in her second year, Howard on the Upper West Side—and my father was worried. My brother, especially, had been broke for many years. He was a two-bit, losing gambler and my father believed he had ruined his life. The last time we'd seen him, he'd come to New Hampshire to purchase a car, a dark blue Dodge Dart with a passenger side window that wouldn't close, and he'd brought a friend up with him named Mitch, who'd wipe his long nose with the back of his hand. My mother, who was still in the house at that time, had offered Mitch some lemonade, but Mitch had refused, made some quiet excuses. It was just a few months after this that my mother left the house for good, and I suppose I've always connected the incidents: the bright afternoon and Mitch slumping in the wicker chair; my mother, who went off to be an actress in New York.

By the time the elevator arrived on his floor, Howard had already unlatched the door and put his head out. I was happy to see he looked good. His complexion was no longer sluggish and his eyes were bright.

"How was the trip?" he inquired.

"Take my bag," I replied.

He was wearing plain khaki pants and a clean blue oxford shirt. As he walked back into the foyer, I thought he resembled Paddington Bear, looking for someone to tell him what to do.

"What's the verdict?" he asked as he waved his thick hand in the air. The kitchen was closet-sized, but the rest of the apartment was spacious. The master bedroom had its own bathroom and a bed decked out in dark green sheets. On the duvet, there was a bright depiction of a safari scene, and I thought to myself that the bed would be big enough to sleep an elephant if the necessity ever presented itself. Howard then led me into the small corner guest room where I'd be sleeping. A large bank of windows on two sides of the room afforded a clear view of the bustling city corner down below.

"It's really nice, Howard," I said after a considered pause. I was thirteen years old and I doled out my compliments accordingly.

"Well, *thank* you," he replied, rummaging around in his pants pocket and pulling out a fist-sized roll of $100 bills. "To celebrate your approval, we're going shopping." At this, he darted past a frumpy leather lounger, unlocked the door, and waved me on. "We can put your stuff away later. C'mon."

Across the street from my brother's new building was a fashionable boutique called Charivari. I had noticed it on my way in because Annie would talk about it incessantly over the phone when she called me from school. Though it was far too expensive for her collegiate budget, she liked to fantasize about their biannual sales, and I was receptacle enough for her reveries. The store felt both spare and sumptuous at once. It was a small space, but immaculately kept. The racks were only halfway filled, each item in its special place. When I first set eyes on the merchandise, I hardly dared touch it, it looked so pure and clean.

As I gazed, Howard followed along, telling me repeatedly that he wanted me to have anything I liked. After some minutes of wandering the store in circles, unable to focus on the task at hand, a white linen blouse caught my eye. The buttons were made of a clear glass and glinted prettily in the light. I looked at the price tag—$400—and recoiled. I imagined my father somewhere over my shoulder, shaking his head in disapproval. My mother was behind the other shoulder, shrieking at the top of her lungs that if Howard would ever bother to take *her* shopping (which of course he *never* would) and if he *ever* offered to buy her anything at all, well then, she'd damn well take him up on it. I stared at the blouse for a very long time and with a terrible longing. A wispy salesman even asked me if I'd like to start a dressing room, but I couldn't do it.

"I mean it," Howard insisted. "Anything at all. That's what money's for." I gazed up at his eager face and thought of all the blouses that I'd ruined in my life. As I was about to tell him that it wasn't any use, I noticed a plain pair of sunglasses in the display case at the front of the store. They had thick square lenses and a functional design. The only thing that made them worthy of their place at Charivari was the fact that they were green—a very pretty green, like the sea.

"They're made of tortoiseshell," the salesman said, picking them out of the case. When I took the glasses in my hands, I glanced furtively at the price tag—$100—still too much, but before I could replace them, Howard had paid, snapping a single green bill from his roll.

When we got outside the store, I asked Howard the one question that none of us in the family had been able to answer. How had he gotten his hands on so much money? He explained to me that, since his first days playing poker in New York, he'd risen through the limits till he made it to the highest staked table in the city: the $50–$100 game at the Mayfair Club. "If I'm beating my table," he told me, the rush-hour traffic pooling around us, "I stand to make about fifty dollars, maybe even a hundred an hour—that's a lot." I accepted his answer. It was the answer we'd all guessed at, even contrary to our worst expectations, but it was only one half of the truth.

• • •

As we walked in the apartment, the phone started ringing. It was someone named "Z," who I gathered was some sort of business associate. "I've got to run an errand and you'll have to come with," Howard said. We then hopped a cab to the Mayfair, near Gramercy Park.

I try now to remember what I thought about the game of poker back then, when I was thirteen, and I suppose it must have seemed awfully mysterious. Though my father dabbled in it, playing for quarters in a faculty game at the school where he taught, and though Annie had watched Howard play and had come to understand the game quite well, the family as a whole regarded it as vulgar—good enough for con men and their ilk, but certainly not good enough for us. It was, in other words, no bridge, and so, even though the family itself may have been composed of a poor moral fiber, we looked down our noses at poker.

My personal view of the game changed when I walked into the Mayfair, however. The walls were as yellow as old lemon rinds and the short charcoal carpeting was sullied and worn, but the majority of the clientele was sparkling. Howard's table, which was in the far corner of the main room, was the only exception, for it was the proverbial "biggest game in town" and a magnet for professional players, who liked to wear sateen and sweats.

"Is Z here?" Howard asked, as we sidled up to the table. It was early for a game of poker on a Sunday night, and there were only four people playing: a slight fellow named Mickey, who was wearing a sweatband around his mop of yellow hair (and bore an uncanny resemblance to the tennis star Björn Borg); a swarthy man named Billy Horan (who'd originally invited Howard to join the game); and a very stiff Orthodox rabbi—the sucker (even I could see that).

According to Mickey, Z had been there earlier, but he'd had to go. "He left a package with Erik for you," he said, eyeing his cards.

"Where's Erik?"

"He's in the john." Mickey chucked some of his chips on the table. It was the first time I'd seen poker chips up close, and I remember thinking they looked like Necco wafers.

"Raise," said Mickey.

"Call," said the rabbi.

Before we'd arrived, Billy (who was the acting dealer for the round) had already placed three cards in the center of the table—an ace of clubs, a king of spades, and a four of hearts. I didn't know the rules of poker, and I doubted Howard would appreciate my asking him questions just then, so I watched. After Mickey raised and the rabbi called, another card was placed faceup in the middle of the table—an eight of spades.

"Bet," said the rabbi.

"Raise," said Mickey.

"Raise you back," said the rabbi. Mickey hesitated.

"Call," he finally said, adjusting his sweatband so it rested on the crown of his head.

Erik then emerged and came toward the table. He was lanky and tall with a great beaky nose, big brown eyes, and thick brows. "You must be Howard's sister," he said, presenting his hand.

"I don't know who you are," I said.

"I'm Erik Seidel. I'm a friend of your brother's." He asked me how I liked New York, what I thought about poker. I told him that I liked it all OK, and that it beat staying home for vacation. He laughed and said I'd fit right in. "Just like your brother." He leaned over and pulled a crumpled paper bag from beneath his chair. "Z left you this," he said. Howard took the bag and looked inside.

"Why can't Z give me a real bag to carry this stuff around in?"

"Dunno," said Erik, settling back into his seat and fixing his eyes on the game.

"All right, let's see what you got," said Mickey.

The rabbi showed his lucky hand—a pair of fours; with the four that was already on the table, they made three of a kind. "Can you beat trips?" he asked. Mickey shook his head.

Billy started laughing. "Trips are for kids," he said.

"Not for silly rabbis," Howard muttered as he walked toward the door. I tagged along, waving good-bye to all the strange new people.

The rabbi glared up at us with astringent disapproval. "You turn out better than your brother, little girl," he said, pulling in his pile of chips. "You don't want to end up in a place like this with people like us."

After driving up Third Avenue, past blocks and blocks of the city's poshest housing, we arrived at a tony address on the Upper East Side. Unlike Howard's building, which had all the charm of a high-rise made of Legos, this building was old—at least a hundred years. The doorman was expecting Howard.

"Mr. Digges didn't say anything about a girl," he said.

"This is my sister," Howard said.

The doorman stared. "All right," he replied. "Elevator's over there."

"We're going to the penthouse," Howard whispered, as if we were going straight to heaven.

When the elevator doors opened, we disembarked in a vast, vaulted hallway, decorated by little more than a crimson Oriental runner. The entire place smelled of orchids and liquor, and I inhaled the aroma deeply. I imagined that only the most rarefied and discerning creature could occupy such a place, and all my inhibitions fairly melted with the pleasure of it. On a table to our right there was a tiny jade Buddha and a vase stuffed with lucky prosperity vines.

"Digges must replace these every other day," my brother mumbled. "They never dry out."

While my brother admired the vines, an ugly little man appeared dark in the doorway and ushered us into the living room. He was squat and rotund, clad in nothing more than a sleeveless white T-shirt and a pair of khaki shorts, which exposed his veiny, dimpled legs. His feet were as bare as a baby's, and his head was perfectly and blindingly bald.

"Hey, Digges," Howard said, offering up the bag. "I hope this helps."

"Sorry to bring you here on such short notice," Digges replied. "But I needed the cash and the banks are all closed. I presume this is the little sister?"

Howard gave me an appraising look. "She's here for the week—on vacation from the eighth grade, if you believe it."

"Jesus," said Digges, whistling. "Eighth grade. That's a real *vintage* year."

"I'm going to go to boarding school next year," I said, eager to impress the charming Digges.

"Boarding school," Digges replied, stooping over a bit to reach my level. "That's something else."

I nodded my head.

"Would you like a little sherry?"

"I'm not sure," I said, blushing, and I knew at that moment that I didn't belong—not there, in that apartment at that hour. There was a large square glass table in the center of the room, and I imagined crawling stealthily beneath it, looking up through the clear wedge of glass at my brother and Digges, who were laughing, who were passing all that money back and forth.

1 ♠ Faces

Until that strange year, that first year that my mother was gone from the house, that first year that I found out my brother played cards and bet sports for a living, the five of us had lived on the campus of St. Paul's, an Episcopal boarding school where my father taught English to the children of the well-to-do. It was an old school, founded in 1855 and modeled after the old English public schools, like Eton and Westminster. Though we'd always lived well, even richly, my family simply didn't belong. We were, in the end, at the mercy of the school, which paid for our housing, our heating, our three meals a day. Unlike many of the other faculty, who had themselves gone to the school and had returned after college to teach—who were, of their own accord, wealthy—my father was of no fancy background, and this was a source of some embarrassment to me.

We were also set apart by what the neighbors perceived as our questionable values, a perception that wasn't altogether unfounded. In the years just before she decided to leave, my mother had taken to drinking quite a bit, a fact I've always seen as a primary cause of what would happen to the family later on. The drinking. The games. Not only our versions of Oh, Hell and chess, but also the marking of bottles and the searching through deep bureau drawers.

The drinking. The games. I remember the day I first saw a connection. How one was like the other in a way. It was the end of the school year, a breezy spring morning, and I was watching my mother through the sliding door that faced out on the courtyard where I liked to play. She had come down the stairs and was sitting demurely in her flannel Lanz nightie on the green and blue plaid couch. In front of her, on an octagonal pine table, sat a glass of Vat 69, her favorite brand of scotch, and a ragged deck of cards. My mother loved her solitaire, and would often spend entire days playing its several varieties, each of which she had to win before she'd move on to the next. On some days, the cards would run badly and she'd force herself to sit there, on the green and blue plaid couch, until the cards fell into proper place.

As the morning hours passed, my mother would shuffle and cry. I wanted to do something, but I was afraid that she'd be angry if she knew that I was watching her, so I continued to spy on her while I played with Kathaleen, my favorite doll. Kathaleen was ten, two years older than I was. She had stringy brown hair and a tattered purple dress, and if you threw her in the air, she made a choking sound. It was the only sound she was able to make and I decided one day that she was deaf. I didn't know sign language, but I would improvise and sit for hours wiggling my fingers in her face.

Though I now understand why my mother was crying, I didn't understand when I was young, so I just sat with Kathaleen, making up stories, explaining to her that my mother (her grandmother) was sad and that when she stopped crying, we'd go inside and sit on her lap. She didn't stop crying, however, and as the clock ticked on to noon, I became a little frightened.

I undid the latch on the door, opened it, and walked into the house.

"It's OK, Mom, I'm here," I said. My mother smoothed her nightie and wiped her swollen eyes.

"I didn't know you were awake," she said.

I jumped on her lap and then signed to Kathaleen, prompting my mother to giggle. I wrapped my arms around her neck, which was warm and smooth against my wrists, and asked her what the matter was. She looked at me, her eyes glassy and unblinking, and started to sob. I didn't know what I had done, so I let go of my mother and began signing again to Kathaleen, telling her that her grandmother wasn't feeling very well and that we should go outside to play. I got up off my mother's lap, walked to the screen door, and slid it open.

"You don't have to go away," my mother said. I stood there and stared at her. I didn't want to make her cry again.

"I'm leaving anyway. I'm tired," she said, going up to her bed.

My mother was an odd creature. She was possessed of a frenetic sort of spirit and there was an effervescence about her that was especially appealing to children. I think that she was not quite of this world, and the part of her that seemed always to be seeking aperture in fact, trying desperately to flee the hardest truths of life, was the part that children loved. She had inquisitive brown eyes, and would often spend her days in a state of frowsiness, her nightgown billowing off her like some academic robe. Her greatest attribute was also her greatest weakness. Her whimsical, curious nature had led her down a dark road.

There was a pertinence to her habit. She hailed from a long line of heavy drinkers. When I was about three, she'd come down with a severe disease of the liver that compounded her problem, and I can vaguely remember she looked something like a ghost, but stained with yellow, as if God had taken a tremendous drag off a cigarette, put my mother up to his lips, and exhaled.

After an especially difficult night, racked by pain and vitiated by fever, she'd stopped thrashing and been still. The doctor had come. He'd taken her arm up in his hands and given her a shot. I'd watched all of this in the mirror that faced my mother's bed, pretending not to notice what was going on. As the doctor was leaving the room, he whispered in my mother's ear that if she didn't stop the drinking it would kill her.

In spite of the doctor's warning, she continued to drink, and this made it difficult to know whether or not she would remember a conversation or keep an appointment. If we wanted to be sure something would stick, we had to repeat it again and again. My sister and brother began what would become a regular campaign against her drinking. They would corner her, make her promise not to drink, and then punish her when she broke her promise, which she inevitably did. The more often they did this, the more clandestine her habit became, and she'd taken to doing her drinking in private.

All the things that she'd done on that morning as I'd watched from the courtyard had been normal. The unhappy looks as she'd take her small sips, the mechanical playing of cards. What had been unusual was what I'd witnessed before my mother had come down the stairs. I'd woken up early and padded down the hallway past my brother's room. His door had been open and I'd walked furtively inside, verifying that he was really awake at such an early hour. Seeing that he wasn't there, I'd gone downstairs to find him.

From the foyer, I could hear my father and my brother speaking quietly in the kitchen. I walked to the doorway and peered through it, just at the corner, so I could see what they were doing. My brother was crouching in front of my mother's liquor cabinet, a roll of Scotch tape in his hand. He'd pulled out all of her bottles—there must have been ten or so—and was marking the level on each with a sliver of the tape. My father was shaking his head and saying that he thought it was unfair for Howard to be doing this. Trust, he said, was the foundation of any family. My brother looked up, his face pasty and moon-shaped, and told my father that the bottles were contraband to begin with. "I'm not rifling through her underwear drawer or anything like that," he said.

My brother was the stealthiest member of the family. Quiet and reserved, he was also overweight, and his extra girth made him invisible. The lines of his face were obscured by the fat, and his eyes were very dark and very difficult to read. I was hardly frightened of my brother when I was eight years old, not because he wasn't a threat, but rather because he barely noticed me. I came up to his stomach when I was eight. He would place his wide palm on my forehead and laugh as I tried to take swipes at his jiggling belly.

The hours that passed between my mother's going up the stairs and the inevitable fight that ensued when my father and brother returned to the house are less vivid in my memory—periods of waiting always are. I remember looking in the cabinet, at the bottle my mother had drawn from, finding a larger, similarly colored bottle, and pouring some measure of its contents in a mug. I walked to the sink, filled the mug up with some water, and then poured the mix into the bottles until their levels reached the appropriate marks. Before completing the task, I weighed the consequences in my mind, unsure as to which was the scarier prospect: that my mother would see that I'd watered her liquor down, or that my brother would discover that my mother had been drinking. I decided that my mother would never think that I had been the one to water the liquor down; she'd think that Annie or Howard had been pilfering, so I screwed the caps onto the bottles as tightly as I could, shoved them back into the cabinet, and went into the television room to retrieve Kathaleen. I hoisted myself onto the green and blue plaid couch and signed frantically in her face.

After sitting like this for some time, I hopped off the couch and decided to go over to the Gracies' house, where my best friend, Johnny, lived. The Gracies lived in the same dormitory complex that we did. It had been erected in the 1960s and housed three separate dorms, two for boys and one for girls. I remember scavenging in the dormitory rooms after the students departed at the end of the year. I would find all sorts of things in those rooms, rich people's things: cast-off pearl necklaces, taffeta scarves, expensive perfumes. I would pick them up and stuff them into a tattered canvas bag, pretending that I was a bandit. Sometimes I'd go with Johnny and we'd comb the dorm rooms systematically and divvy up the spoils at night. I remember especially well a trip we made to one of the girls' dorms. We'd pulled out one of the particle-board desk drawers and discovered a keep of unused tampons. Johnny had turned his head away, embarrassed by the sight, while I'd stared intently, perplexed by the paper-wrapped goodies.

The Gracies' house was an exact architectural replica of ours, but it was on the opposite side of the complex and everything about it was backwards. While our kitchen window faced out on the muddy bank of one of the campus ponds (over which an amputated tree, a stump, stretched miserably), the Gracies' kitchen faced out on the esplanade where the campus chapel stood. There was more light in the Gracies' house, or at least that is how I remember it, and more warmth. Most of all, there were the Gracies themselves. They were a kindly, sociable bunch, freckled and well fed. Mrs. Gracie had a broad, honest face and jovial brown eyes. She would tell me I was the daughter she never had, lift me up onto her lap, and stroke my greasy, unkempt hair. Her benignly affectionate gestures made me wince with uncomfortable pleasure. I was too young to have anything but the most powerful ardor for my mother, and to accept kindness from anyone else seemed a betrayal.

• • •

If I'd been smart, I would have phoned my mother and told her I wanted to stay at the Gracies' overnight. It would have been an easy way to keep out of the family fray. I was not especially smart about such things, however, and I worried that if I stayed at the Gracies', I'd miss out on the evening's events. I don't mean to imply that I enjoyed those evenings, each of which stung brightly as a new laceration; rather, what I relished was the *togetherness* that came with total family conflict. When my mother and father began an argument, you could see their love blaze hot across their faces; and if all five of us got involved in the fracas, the effect would be narcotic, knocking us out.

I knocked on the door before reentering our house. It seemed like a reasonable precaution at the time. No one answered, so I walked quietly into the foyer. It was just after dusk, and the only sounds were the cicadas and the occasional whoop from a student in the dorm. I pressed Kathaleen close to my chest and walked up the stairs to check on my mother. When I got there, her room was dark. There was a small square window on one side of the room and a large rectangular window on the other, both of them shielded by thick burlap curtains. I stared at her for a very long time, adjusting my eyes to the absence of light, wanting to warn her that the rest of the family would be home soon. I touched her clammy forehead with my hand and whispered, "Mama, mama."

She mumbled something that I couldn't make out and rolled over. I got into bed with her and wrapped my arms around her hips. I buried my face in her chest and whispered again, "Mama, mama."

Images streaked through my head of the three of them coming up the stairs and charging through the door to her room. They'd snap on the overhead light and proceed to browbeat her until she admitted she was drunk. I was just about to shake her awake, but then I thought better of it. I was afraid she would ask me why I hadn't told her before—or, worse, why I hadn't stopped my brother from marking her bottles to begin with—and I couldn't stand the thought of being implicated. I'd always been beyond blame in the family's disputes, and I guarded this privilege with extreme vigilance. It was as if I had a surplus of innocence and was hoarding it for the day I'd be forced to take action. The more innocence I accrued, the logic went, the less guilty I'd be in some rancorous future.

That night, watching my mother sleep, her face ivory and serene, I decided to leave things as they were. I got up from the bed, brushed my hair to the side, and walked into my room, which was just down the hallway. I sat on my bed and looked out the window. Across the oval pond stood a large stone library where the boarding school students would go after dinner to study. It blazed with a wonderful light that would shimmer over the corrugated water. I had stared out that window for years, watching the students come and go, envying their independence, dreaming of the day when I'd become one of them, happily ensconced in a clean, sterile dorm room, away from the mess in the house.

After a seemingly interminable period of anxious waiting, I heard the click of the front door, followed by my brother's footfalls. When I got downstairs, he was standing in the kitchen, shoving potato chips into his mouth. His hair was slicked back so you could see his wide forehead and his small, nut-brown eyes. They were the facsimile of my eyes.

I stared at him.

"What?" he asked.

"Nothing."

"You want some chips?" The bag crinkled in his hands. Everything was so unbearably quiet that the sound startled me. Howard stood motionless, examining my face.

"What's the matter?"

"Nothing."

He glanced at the liquor cabinet. I heard more footfalls, this time my father's.

"We shouldn't do this in front of her," my father said.

I scuttled into the hallway and stood just out of sight.

There was the sound of the cabinet being opened, then the clink of the bottles.

"She moved them," my brother said, grimly.

"They do look a bit disturbed," my father said.

When I finally got up to her room, breathless after climbing two flights of slippery stairs in my stocking feet, she was lying in bed just as she had been. I shook her as hard as I could.

"I'm asleep," she mumbled.

"Get up—please," I said.

Her eyes were fuzzy and indistinct.

I heard my father coming up the stairs and bolted out the door. He passed me in the hallway, his body was as taut as a bow and I was afraid of him.

I ran back downstairs and waited in the foyer on a small maple bench. There was a very large lithograph on the wall showing a group of men in tight red suits, marauding the countryside, hunting rabbits. The rabbits looked frightened, their eyes watery and desperate, running scattershot across the hills. Behind the picture, a large switchboard controlled the circuit breakers and fuses for the entire dormitory complex. Whenever there was a fire alarm, either my mother or my father would run to the lithograph and yank it off the wall, exposing the fuses. As children will do, I had at some point surmised that the lithograph had been selected to cover the fuse box precisely because it portended some vague, though incomparably horrible, doom.

My mother and father then appeared at the top of the stairs. They looked very small. They were holding each other tightly, like Jacob and the angel. After some wrangling, my mother broke loose and streaked down to the landing.

My brother then emerged from the kitchen, defiantly striding to the base of the stairwell, swiveling the bottle in the air. When my mother saw him brandishing the half-full bottle, she turned around, but my father was just above her. She had nowhere to go and she collapsed, like a fallen cake, her nightie gathering around her chest and knees.

"You watered it down," my brother said.

"What are you talking about?" my mother cried, shaking her head. "What are you talking about?"

My brother continued to swivel the bottle in her face.

"I marked it."

My mother wheeled herself around then, toward the door, and disappeared. Like some royal retinue, all of us followed, my father first, mortified that she'd done what none of us had ever dared to do: leave the private confines of our house and step out onto campus, where the enormous dormitory windows blinked like disapproving eyes. My brother and sister and I trailed behind. Once the cool springtime air hit my face, my vision lurched. I could see only my father and mother, struggling by the campus post office, and the lights of the library across the pond shining brightly on their faces.

2 ♠ Stealing

But maybe I should start a little smaller, the way most gamblers start. Maybe I should start with the inside of my mother's purse, a worn-out leather satchel that sagged from the arm of one of the kitchen chairs. Inside one could discover an entire world: crinkly silver gum wrappers, salmon-pink lipstick and plum-colored rouge, twice-read and ravaged old mystery novels (Agatha Christie, Simenon), a pack of Merit cigarettes, a book of ragged checks, a loosened roll of Certs, and sometimes a present for me that had slipped her mind, a key chain or Smurf. At the very center of it all, weighty as a dumbbell, was her wallet. If the purse was like a dump, the wallet was a landfill, with credit cards galore and pictures of the children stuffed into the torn plastic sheaves. It was a typical wallet, made of imitation leather with a distressed button snap. There was also an exterior change purse, which clicked when it shut. I can vividly remember making trips to the local market with my mother, her taking out that behemoth wallet, snapping it and clicking it, pulling out a pen and clicking that, writing a check or signing a credit card slip, saying thank you, then shoving that bulging apparatus back into her purse.

I was usually able to tell if my mother was gone by checking to see if the purse was in the kitchen. If it was on the couch in the television room, I would know that she'd come home, but that she'd gone off to a neighbor's or her bedroom in a hurry. She didn't like to leave her purse sitting on the couch like that; it would lose its shape and gape open like a mouth, its contents spilling out onto the plaid. On occasion, if I knew she was gone, I'd rifle through the purse, filching a Certs, placing it gingerly onto the tip of my tongue like a Communion wafer. I hardly dared disturb much of anything else. This isn't to say that I was all innocent; I was simply too young to ascertain the value of an open and highly disorganized purse, a value that my siblings understood innately. I can very clearly remember the rather funny image of my brother leaning over the couch in the television room, his hand buried deep in the satchel. He would start if I came upon him. "You're not going to tell Mom about this, are you?" he'd say. "Because if you do, I *will* have to kill you."

Whether or not any money had been stolen, the contents of the wallet would need to be replenished on a regular basis, and negotiations between my father and mother over how much he should give her would take on a tense and attenuated air. My father would stiffen at the mere mention of money, and whenever my mother would ply him for cash, his demeanor would take on a smirking and sharp-edged expression of incredulity. "I thought I gave you a twenty just yesterday," he'd say. Or: "Do you always have to spend every last penny?" We children would watch from the doorway, observing the heated exchange. Our mother would invariably rearrange her features into the picture of a begging little girl (with the bullet eyes of Little Orphan Annie, I remember thinking) while our father would grow gruff and impatient. There was really no remedying it. My mother and father were as opposite in their attitudes about money as two people could possibly be, and their constant fighting about the subject served only to push them further and further into their respective corners until they resembled nothing more than caricatures of themselves.

There was, of course, good reason for my father to be so mad; half gallons of scotch were not cheap, and my mother consumed them at a fairly rapid clip. It had long been a tacit agreement between the two of them that he wouldn't ask, but that she shouldn't buy, and so their conversations were like an embroidery, laced with delicate deceptions. "The steaks cost nearly twice what I thought when I went to the market yesterday. Can I have an extra ten dollars?" my mother would ask, and my father, if he was feeling up to it, would mount an extraordinary effort, pressing as hard as he could against the lie, but being finally unable to budge it. It was, no matter its lack of verity, opaque as dirty glass, and the longer he tried to see through it, the more he saw himself—a lifelong teetotaler who was finally unable to face, let alone understand, my mother's problem.

If Howard was stealthy about stealing from my mother's purse, Annie was rather more shrewd, and I can remember her watching such scenes in the kitchen, her eyes glowing green with an intricate design. The logical time to steal from the purse was, of course, just after it had been replenished, but not before some part of its contents had been spent, and Annie would wait until just after my mother returned from some trip into town to make her move.

I can remember one evening in particular. It was the winter vacation, a stinging frigid day, and my mother and I had spent the better part of the afternoon shopping. We'd started out at Souther's, the upscale market where my mother bought our food. It was a ramshackle, quaint little shop just a few miles down the road, and my mother loved chatting with the cashiers there about what was in season. In the middle of the winter in New Hampshire, of course, nothing at all is in season, and so she made do with some wilted, washed-out spinach, a sack of mealy apples, and an impossibly delectable-looking Entenmann's chocolate cake. We walked out to our little orange Renault 5, our feet crunching through the icy banks, and then drove more deeply into town, to the tailor's on Main Street. My mother needed to pick up a dress at the tailor's and so I'd waited outside in the car, making little marks on the window with my finger, mumbling absently to myself, eagerly anticipating the shop we'd go to next. It was, I knew, inevitable: the liquor store.

Just down a small incline from the city's wholesome Main Street, to the right of the Zayre's and across the dirty parking lot from the bus terminal, the liquor store was a bureaucratic-looking structure, rigid and clean in its motifs. It reminded me vaguely of the Hall of Justice, the place where the Superfriends congregated every Saturday morning to catch the week's toughest villain, and so, even though I knew that what my mother bought there was poison, I regarded it as hallowed ground.

"Do you want to come in?" my mother asked. She had a plastic look, the expression of a person so possessed by some unbearable necessity that it appeared as if her face might snap in two. She didn't want me to come in, I knew that. I think she had no idea how much I enjoyed the inside of that liquor store—the orderly and sterile endless rows, each bottle in its place, cataloged and kept track of. I relished the way those bottles would clink as they rolled back and forth in the bottom of the cart. It was, to my childish and, by this time, frozen ears, the exact sound of money.

"No," I said. "I'll just wait in the car."

As we drove up to the curb in front of the dormitory complex, I could see that not a single light was on, a sure sign that our father had gone out. (Whenever he left the house, he would turn off all the lights, a useless attempt at household thrift, seeing as the school paid the electricity bill.) A powdery glow sifted out from the television room window, however, and when we came in the door, there was Annie, sitting on the carpet in front of the TV. Her naked, pale legs were splayed out in a V, an ordered game of solitaire between them. It was her habit to sit like that, in the grainy blue light, playing cards on the floor or just staring into space. As my mother and I emerged from the entranceway, our faces flushed with sudden warmth, Annie started.

"How'd it go?" she asked. Her tiny square nose was nestled pertly in her bone white face. She was twelve then. I was five.

"Fine," our mother said, loosening her jacket. "Why do you ask?"

"Just wondering," Annie replied, lowering her eyes.

"You can put the black seven on the red eight—over there. You see?" our mother said, putting the bags on the wing chair and kneeling down beside her.

"Did I ask for your help?" Annie said, putting the card in its place.

"No," our mother said. She stood up, grabbed the bags off the chair, and went to the kitchen to put their contents away.

I remained in the room, lingering by the dusty Zenith.

"Where did everybody go?"

"Dunno," said Annie.

"Can I watch you play your game?"

"I guess."

"Can I turn on the light?"

"No."

We then heard a sound from the kitchen—the icy clink of some bottles being shifted, then a cabinet clicking shut.

"Did she go to the store?" Annie said, looking straight at me.

"I don't know."

"Yes you do."

"No I don't."

"Well, what were you doing that whole time then? Picking your nose?"

"No."

"Did you go in with her?"

"Where?" I replied.

"*Where*? You know, Katy, you really suck at lying."

When she finished with her game, Annie got up off the dingy white carpet and went up to her bedroom—to wait. She lived all alone on the second floor, to the right of the parlor, a large expanse of air and light with a floor-to-ceiling window that faced out on the center of the campus. Every Christmastime, my mother and father would erect a ten-foot tree in front of the window, festooning it with lights and silvery balls.

Because Annie had the whole floor to herself, complete

with a miniature kitchen, I regarded her as a bit of a princess. She had an antique queen-sized bed and matching dresser. She even had her own bathroom and shower, an unimaginable luxury it seemed to me then, seeing as I was forced to share my bathroom with Howard, who wasn't particularly clean.

After Annie went up to her room without a word, my mother remained in the kitchen. She'd started her own game of solitaire, and was hunched over the long pine table. I didn't see her drink that night, but somehow, as if by a special osmosis, she became increasingly slow in her movements as the evening progressed. I was sitting cross-legged on the couch, listening to the slap of the cards from the kitchen. I lay down, smelled the fabric, which was rich with the odor of cigarette smoke, then sat up again and leaned against a ragged blue pillow. It seems to me in retrospect that a great anticipation suffused the evenings of my youth; I was biding my time, and I can vividly recall the thought, which looped through my mind like some overwrought sound track, that it was merely a matter of waiting—that someday, soon enough, both my brother and sister would be off to the boarding school and I'd be alone.

My mother came into the room then, listing for a moment in the doorway before fluttering down on the couch. "Hello, my lovely," she slurred, lighting up a Merit. "We *did* have a wonderful day today, didn't we?"

"Yes."

"And we got a lot done today, too."

"Yes."

"I wonder where your father could be. I think I'll lie down here and wait for him to get home. Would you turn up the TV?"

"Sure," I said, scurrying over to the television set and ratcheting up the volume. I waited there for a couple of minutes, until she fell asleep. Then I walked back to the couch, pulled the glowing red stick from her fingers, and stubbed it out.

· · ·

It must have been late. I was watching the late-edition news, sitting by my mother on the green and blue plaid couch. The sighs she'd emit when she'd rearrange her body in her sleep were as familiar and soothing as anything else, a quiet sort of comfort on a dark wintry night, no one awake besides Annie, who was still in her room, listening to *Grease*. (I could hear the bass line spilling down the stairs.) But then, as if in hologram, she was there, standing in the hallway, her body lit up by the TV's white glow. She had a strong body, compact and tightly muscled. When younger, she'd been a talented gymnast, and I remember my father waking early and taking her to meets. I would sometimes tag along and watch her swing from bar to bar, watch the chalk fly off her hands before it settled on the floor. In all my recollections of Annie, she's the toughest of us all—confident and blunt. She had a way of talking that was just this side of taunting, a clipped, carousing voice that would carry through a room. In retrospect, my sister was like a second mother to me, though I was hard put to admit this at the time. She'd try to give me discipline, and sometimes she'd brush out my hair, but I'd rebuff her. I had my own mother, after all, and besides that, I was stubborn. Our parents attributed our difficult relationship to Annie's place in the birth order. She was, they liked to remind me, the middle child. "That's why she's so determined," they'd say. Whatever the cause, she could be fierce, and when I saw her in the doorway, still clad in white T-shirt and undies, I balked.

"Is she asleep?" she whispered.

"I don't know," I said. She stood for just a moment, her head cocked to the side. I remember the way the light from the television rayed across her cheek. I could make out only one of her eyes and a single and archly raised eyebrow.

She walked to the kitchen, where she rummaged around in the dark. I could hear the sharp snap of the wallet clicking shut, then the crinkling of money.

By the time my father got home, I'd curled up with my mother on the green and blue plaid couch, square in her stomach, like a joey. He closed the door and hit the lights.

"Get up," he said, shaking us. "Rise and shine!" My mother raised her body up, recomposing her face and her hands. I tumbled off the couch, ran over to my father, started jumping all over him. When I looked at my mother from his vantage point, I could see she was fine. There wasn't any need to distract him.

"Hi," she said. "Where have you been?"

"I was out with our friend Steven. You remember him?" my father said, leaning on the armchair by the window. "Hey, can I ask you a favor?"

"Sure."

"I ran out of money. Do you have any left from this afternoon?"

"Sure," my mother said, getting up off the couch. She went into the kitchen and looked in her purse.

Silence.

"Did you touch the purse, Katy?"

"No."

"Did Annie?"

"No," I said, not daring to give any further explanation. My sister's dim appraisal of my talent for deception still hung in my ears.

"No? Are you sure about that?" she said crossly.

"No," I said again, shaking my head. "*No*."

I could dramatize things further. Describe to you the way my mother folded in her chair, the way my father's face turned dark and mean as offal, but all of these stories seem the same to me now, there's really no use in repeating them.

I suppose, in the end, it would have been possible to divine everything that would happen to the family in the next twenty years just by looking at that bulbous leather purse. It was the palimpsest of some oddball notion. A notion of wealth. Or of freedom. Credit cards and charge accounts, long overdue. Squandered money. Petty. I guess a kind of nothingness.

I think we had come to believing that money was equivalent to happiness.

3 ♠ Games

If money was what kept us at a distance from one another, then the playing of games was what brought us together. When all five of us gathered at the sticky pine table to play cards (our favorites were Hearts and Oh, Hell), I'd almost always lose, but I didn't really mind. No matter what might happen in the game, I'd get to sit around our kitchen table, nestled snugly between my mother and sister, listening to their chirruping voices as they called out their tricks. My brother and father would sit at either end of the table in their chairs, their eyes rolling coolly in their sockets. This was as close as the family ever got, and so, even though the lot of us were sometimes violently competitive (if Annie lost a game, she'd throw the cards; and if Howard lost, he'd glare as if you'd insulted his deepest, most delicate part, then slink around the kitchen like a very proud cat), the atmosphere would seem to me incomparably congenial. Somewhere along the line I'd gotten it into my head that the playing of games was the same thing as civility and that friendly competition was the closest thing to love we'd ever know.

Though my view of things was certainly exaggerated, it had its family precedent. Our parents had fallen in love over a game of cards. It was a story our mother loved to tell, and it had lodged in our minds like a shrapnel. They were both students at the Harvard Graduate School of Education and my mother had secured a room close to campus. When she got to the top of the stairs, melting in the heat, she saw our father sitting at a table with her new roommates, playing bridge. He was leaning back in his chair, his cards fanned out in his elegant fingers, so focused on the game that he hardly registered my mother's flustered presence. He had thick blond hair and ebullient blue eyes and, to hear my mother tell it, he was the most beautiful creature she'd ever seen. "I wouldn't mind some help with my luggage," she'd said, and by February of that year (and after countless hands of bridge), they were engaged.

We children were indoctrinated into the family love of games at an early age. As toddlers, we'd been taught the most basic card games—War, Spit, and Go Fish, none of which our father would help us to win, claiming that to do so would constitute poor sportsmanship. We were also affected deeply by our father's infectious love of word games; Rasputin, Inky Pinky, and all manner of punning were ubiquitous in the household, providing respite from the spirit-tamping chaos of the days. If he wasn't actively meditating, our father was always available, like a swami in his den, for playing such games, and I remember feeling that the limits of his book-lined walls constituted the full extent of household joy.

Our mother had her own gaming preferences, which, though not as high-spirited as our father's, backed up his insistence that games were of paramount importance. By any account, she was a genius; her IQ was through the roof and her mental acuity was evident even when she was performing the most mundane tasks. She'd astonish me when I was little by reciting aphorisms and odd bits of poetry she'd read years before. And, it would seem, she'd astonish herself as well, covering her mouth with her hand as if a bird had escaped from her lips. I regularly mistook her brilliance for wisdom and was unable to understand how a woman who possessed so much wonderful knowledge could have such a difficult time keeping her life together. When I'd go to the campus dining hall or to other faculty houses, grown-ups would always mention my mother's intelligence, telling me what a marvelously brilliant woman she was, their eyes narrowing to fascinated slits. Their compliments had about them a faintly disapproving air, the assumption being that, like the cliché of the pretty-faced fat person, she was wasting something.

In addition to her love of solitaire, she was a devotee of the *New York Times* crossword puzzle and could finish the Sunday edition in twenty minutes. She would write out her answers in ink as if she were completing a laundry list, hesitation hardly evident in her neatly voluptuous penmanship. There were some terrible days when our father would implore her to enter the national crossword puzzle competitions, sure that she'd win and bring home some extra money, which we sorely needed. Perhaps because she could sense usury in these pleas, or perhaps because she wished to keep her talent private, my mother would always refuse, frustration bursting onto her face.

As an audience to such fights, we children gleaned that intelligence was the most important thing in the world. It was what we should strive for, what we should brag about, it was the defining characteristic of our humanity. Our parents didn't much care whether or not we got good grades in school. Winning at games was what mattered.

One summer day when I was nine, I decided it was high time I learned bridge. My sister, who'd just finished her junior year at the boarding school, was going to New York for the summer, and this meant the family would be needing a fourth. North, South, East, or West, which would I be? The game's very language intrigued me, and I was eager to usurp my sister's place at the long kitchen table, to utter words like *singleton* and *dummy,* which would roll around like marbles in my mouth.

When I walked into the study to ask for my very first lesson, however, my father was meditating. He was lying on the floor, his six-foot four-inch frame extending almost all the way from one end of the room to the other, a small, wet rag placed delicately over his eyes. The rest of his face was lit up freakishly by a sunlamp, under which he'd fry himself for hours at a time. In consequence, his face had grown as shriveled as a raisin and would stay that way, even through the long New England winters.

"Will you teach me bridge now?" I asked. My father started.

"I didn't hear you come in," he said. I knelt down beside him and tugged at the rag (not daring to remove it completely). "I'm tired," he continued. "It's been a very long day with Annie leaving and all. How about tomorrow?"

"Just one lesson," I pleaded.

"I doubt we'll be playing bridge for a while," he said, leaning up against the bookshelf. "But I'll teach you soon—I promise."

"All right," I said, leaving the den and running (as loudly

as I could, so my father could hear that there was sadness in my feet) up the stairs to my room.

• • •

About a week after Annie left for New York City, I was tempted into the dreary little kitchen by the presence of a box of fresh Devil Dogs. When I walked in, I saw my brother and father playing chess at the stained Formica counter. They were both standing up, furiously pounding the chess pieces down. My brother was wearing an overtight Lacoste shirt, and you could see his vestigial breasts pressing up against the fabric. His bangs had grown out, so he had to keep flipping them out of his eyes. My father was wearing a soiled cotton T-shirt and worn tennis shoes. It was his habit to wear a very old pair of madras shorts, which were thinning with age, but which he refused to toss out, at least not until they fell apart completely. Both of them were wearing expressions of extreme fierceness and concentration, and I was afraid to disturb their play. Each time they plunked a piece down, a startling echo would rebound about the room and my nerves would drown. After Howard won the game, he came over to greet me while my father put the pieces away.

Although my brother's trouncing of my father in chess was not an especially difficult moment, at least not as things were going in the household when I was young, I remember it, and almost more vividly than anything else. This is partly because the air of my father's defeat hung heavy over the household for days afterward and partly because my father refused to play my brother in chess ever again. ("Oh, why bother," he'd say if my brother invited him. "We already know who's going to win.") More than anything else, however, I remember the muggy afternoon so clearly because it was after this that my brother left the house for New York City, and though I don't remember the actual day of his departure, I can vividly remember the scene in the kitchen, the solid iron light falling heavy through the curtains, and the terrifying certainty, as if the entire afternoon were a fortune being told, that things in the household would never again be the same.

Before my siblings left, we were all in one house, ineluctably in one another's presence. No matter how competitive or mean we may have been, there wasn't any doubting we were close. With both my siblings gone, however, the house became a ghostly place, and I remember feeling as if the three of us who stayed had to move in slow motion through the torpid summer air. I'd spend most of my days on the couch, lamenting the oppression of it all. (I would, it was clear, never be playing the fourth at bridge.) I suffered from migraines then and would lie prostrate for hours, cogitating on nothing, as if my head were an empty maraca. I would wear a small woolen hat that I'd decided helped with the headaches, and whenever I had to engage with anyone at all, I would literally pull the wool over my eyes.

That summer I spent a great deal of time in the woods behind the house, constructing an elaborate fantasy life for myself. The campus was littered with tall black lampposts like those in *The Chronicles of Narnia,* and I spent countless hours waiting for Mr. Tumnus to whisk me away to another world. My father continued his morning meditations and, in an effort to keep the family afloat financially, taught English and film to the summer school students. My mother was attending nightly summer stock rehearsals for *Guys and Dolls,* and with everyone busy, we paid so little attention to the passage of time that it took us nearly a week to notice that Howard hadn't called. This first week of ignorance soon stretched into two, and my father, not knowing what to do, finally filed a missing persons report. About three weeks into our half-assed family vigil, the police rang us up. My mother, in her nightie, ran into the study.

"Hello?"

"Hello," said a voice. "Is Mr. Lederer at home?"

"No," said my mother. "He's out on an errand. But this is his wife. May I ask who's calling?"

"He'll know who I am, ma'am." (I was, by this time, an expert eavesdropper, adept at dislodging and replacing receivers without a sound.) "Could you just tell him *I need to know the year that Emily Dickinson was born*?"

"What kind of prank caller is this?"

"Not a prank caller, ma'am, just leaving a message for Mr. Lederer."

"Well, good grief," my mother cried. "He *most certainly* knows when Emily Dickinson was born and if this isn't some kind of code, then I don't know what it could be! Good afternoon to you, sir!" She slammed the phone down before wandering into the kitchen, where she took up her place at the table and started to shuffle.

She was still playing cards when my father came home. Hearing the creak of the door, she jumped up.

"Where have you been?"

"At the office."

"There's a message for you."

My father blanched.

"What kind of game is this?"

"All right," my father said, leading my mother to the study. By the time I'd scurried to the door, it was closed. I peeked through the keyhole, which provided only partial views.

"I thought it would upset you if you heard from the police, so I told them to leave me a message in code."

"You don't think I want to know where my son is just as much as you do?"

"But what if the news is bad?"

"Bad, like what? He's chopped up in a Dumpster? He's in the East River? What?"

"You never know."

"You're right, I *never* know because no one in this household thinks I can understand anything at all. I'm not a stupid woman."

"I know."

"I am a *smart* woman, and if you think I don't know what's going on this household, then you're *greatly* mistaken."

"I'll call the police station right now," my father said.

Once he got through, they said that they'd inquired with New York and New Jersey, and no one had heard or seen any trace of Howard. After asking what this meant, he was told that all area hospitals and morgues had been checked, that there was nothing more for them to do. My father said thank you, told the people at the station that it was OK to leave word with his wife ("The Dickinson code is no longer necessary," he said), and hung up.

It's not every day, of course, that a man decides to use the name of a nineteenth-century poet as his code word, but that is exactly what my father did. It was an act that, though perplexing to others, was never perplexing to me. Though he was a high school English teacher, and could have settled into a retiring sort of existence explicating *Catcher in the Rye* for the rest of his days, he'd always been restless, eager to accomplish more. I always suspected his relentless drive had something to do with his Polish mother, a stern, demanding woman with a blond bouffant wig. She'd insisted all along that my father grow up to be a lawyer or doctor, but after completing his first year at Harvard Law, he'd decided to transfer into the education program and become a high school English teacher.

My father's restlessness reached its zenith when I was about four. He'd been teaching at the boarding school for twelve years and had decided to expand his knowledge by pursuing a Ph.D. at the state university. As the time drew near for his oral examinations, which required him to become thoroughly familiar with one hundred American novels, he'd sit in his study for hours, overwhelmed by all the work he had to do. I remember once walking into that study. It had been a difficult night, dinner time spent in such rancor that all five of us ended up sulking over berries and sherbet. My father was sitting in the dark, sobbing. I walked up to him, could hear the soft padding of my feet across the carpet as if they belonged to someone else.

"What do you need, Katy?" he asked. I asked him to tell me a story.

"I'm busy," he said. "I'm sorry I haven't been able to read to you recently, but it's been a difficult summer."

I asked him if I could turn on the light. He told me that he'd rather I didn't. I asked him if I could sit on his lap in the dark and he took me up and held me very close. I asked him what the matter was, and he told me that he had to read too many stories. He had to read them very carefully, had to learn them by rote, he said.

"By rote," I repeated.

"I have to learn them by rote, and then I have to tell some people what I learned. So I've been reading, but the stories are all blending into one another and I'm tired."

"What kind of stories are they?"

"Old stories," he said, "and long. They are very long stories. They are—some of them—very sad stories," he said.

"Why do you read those stories?"

"Because they're important stories. They're very famous stories," he said.

I didn't understand how sad my father was—what it meant to be so sad—so I just sat there in his lap and fell asleep.

I have a picture of me and my father from that time. In it he's teaching me how to ride a bicycle. He's leaning toward me, holding the back of my three-speed Schwinn with one hand, brushing my forearm with the other. I look very small in my salmon pink bathing suit and ragged white tennies. There's something similar in the faces, the same pug nose, the hair combed rakishly to the side. Our eyes are obscured by shadow, deeply set, intent on some point very far down the road. My father looks so young to me, his madras shorts resting loosely on his hips, his short-sleeved shirt still tight around his biceps. He's a hulking man, but he's guiding me with care. The trees in the background furl out behind us like wings.

4 ♠ The Bar Point

It was midday when my father and I arrived in Manhattan in our little orange Renault. The trip to New York City from our town took seven hours, and by the time we entered the Lincoln Tunnel, after speeding all the way, I had a very sore behind and a temporary deafness in one ear. There was no air-conditioning, and, because it was the middle of summer, we'd rolled the windows down for the duration of the trip. Among the taxicabs and limousines, the Renault looked awfully puny, just a two-door with a fragile sloping hood. It was an old car, nearly as old as I was, but it was French, so that in Concord I'd always considered it a fashion statement. In the glamorous city of New York, however, it seemed drab. The exterior paint was flaking as if the car had eczema, the seat belts were broken, and the clutch was blown, but my father loved the little car (it got 32 miles per gallon), and he refused to get rid of it until it outright died. The discomfort of our thrifty ride, combined with our exhaustion, made New York seem dark and out of focus, as if we were seeing it through the small end of a telescope.

It must have been six in the morning or so when my father had woken me up. My room at that time was especially messy (it had royal blue wall-to-wall carpet that was covered in archaeological layers of petrified gum, dirty undies, and pieces of a jigsaw that I'd long ago abandoned but had never put away), and when my father walked in, I was ashamed. His feet were always bare and his toes were long and thin, so that I imagined the gum and the undies and the pieces of the ruined, scattered puzzle lodging themselves between them.

"We're going to New York!" he yelled, his sunburned face grinning. I looked at him blankly, then with frank anticipation. Either Howard was dead, chopped up in a Dumpster, or he wasn't. "I spoke with your sister on the phone," he went on. "She found Howard—ran into him on Seventh Avenue, strangely enough. He was walking toward some club. I guess he found a job and never bothered to call."

"He never bothered to call?"

"He never bothered to call, but he's fine—*he's alive*." My father sighed. "Your mother has to be at her rehearsal for *Guys and Dolls* later on, so you and I are going to go it alone. We're going to go to New York, just you and I! What do you think about that?" My father started rummaging through my bureau drawers, which he'd painted blue and white to match the colors on my headboard. I was really confused. Why, if Howard was OK, did we need to be driving to New York on a Sunday? I looked at my father. His jaw was as tense as rubber bands.

"How about this?" he asked, handing me a pink-checked wrap-around skirt. It was covered in stains and I cringed. My father threw the skirt back in the drawer and rummaged further. "Then this." He held a pair of dark blue jeans to his chest. They were ugly pants, out of fashion (even I knew that), but they were clean, and I wanted very badly to be clean when I got to New York.

When Howard first arrived in the city, he'd stayed with Annie in her summer sublet for a few days before moving into a drug-infested flophouse called the George Washington. He'd then disappeared for several weeks before Annie found him walking down the street. According to her, he was passing out in Washington Square Park in the daytime, then working at some chess club at night. (There were several of these in New York at the time—holes in the wall where the hardest-core players would bet on the games and hang out.) When the weather was wet and he couldn't stand the sopping grass, he'd rent a little room at a hotel called the Regent, the place where he'd agreed to meet up with my father and me. A rundown hotel of the type that was once common in the city but is now fairly rare, the Regent was filthy and cheap, but also oddly grand. It had once been a fashionable destination for socialites and tourists before the neighborhood surrounding it had fallen into disrepair.

When my father and I walked into the lobby, we were greeted with a solid and insurmountable wall of putrescence—some combination of liniment, urine, and must. At the far end of the lobby, in front of a wall of gilded mirrors, stood a short, crooked man in a bright flannel shirt. His eyes seemed too small for their baggy sockets and his nose too large, so that he resembled a basset hound. When we asked for Howard's room, he gave us the number—no questions.

My father and I were unable to discover the elevator, and since my father was too proud to ask the strange man at the desk for its location, we made the exhausting climb up six flights of stairs to Howard's floor. It was a cold, modern stairwell, presumably installed long after the original hotel had been built, and was much less charming. When we finally arrived at Howard's room, I stood stiffly behind my father's legs, watching from beside them. He banged on the door. No answer. We could hear the sound of a television blaring. He banged again, no answer.

"Get the man," my father said, yanking the doorknob.

I ran down the stairs, into the lobby. "I need help," I exclaimed.

"What kind of help?"

"The door won't open, but the TV's on."

The man started pawing through the hotel records.

"No, there's no time," I said, bursting into tears. "*I think he's not waking up.*"

"All right," the man said, dislodging himself from his position behind the desk.

When we got to Howard's room, my father looked sheepishly at the manager. "I'm sorry to trouble you," he said.

"We'll see how sorry you have to be," the man replied, pulling out a key and opening the door. In the far corner of the boxy room, I could make out Howard's back. He was passed out on his stomach, swaddled in yellowing sheets. The casement was rattling. The air was offensively sweet. On the floor was a yellow duffel, which had spilled open to reveal several white T-shirts, a razor, and a small folded chessboard that he'd been given as a good-bye present. My father started shaking Howard, yelling in his face, demanding that he open his eyes.

The next thing I remember, we are standing in the basement of another hotel, the hotel that my brother lived in for the first few weeks he was in New York. My father is handing the manager some money, apologizing for what has happened. This manager, who has a handsome, smiling face, tells my father not to worry about it. His son's a good kid, he says, just unlucky. My father nods. "I know," he says. The light in this basement is swirling so dramatically that I wonder whether it is in fact the real light of that cloudy summer afternoon, or simply the light of recollection, like a filigree holding the memory together. I've looked at it so often, pulled it from the drawer so many times, that it's grown creased, fraying at the edges.

Despite overwhelming evidence, the family ignored my brother's situation with great facility. Even after my father and I had gone to the city to retrieve Howard's belongings, it was as if it never really happened, weren't happening. It was somehow too obvious, like a brutal light that leaves you blind. I remember telling friends at school that my father had paid off my brother's pusher for $10,000. I don't know where I got this story, whether it was true or whether I made it up. Either way, I remember wishing the situation were more epic and less sordid. I wanted it to be like all those other stories I'd heard about legendary gamblers who wore ten-gallon hats and puffed on cigarillos from Savannah.

· · ·

It was not until many years later that I coaxed the whole story out of Howard. We were riding on a train from New York to Connecticut to visit our grandparents. It was wintertime and the other passengers were either sleeping or reading newspapers, so I asked Howard to tell me what it had been like for him that first year in New York.

"Don't you already know the story?" he asked.

"No," I replied. "Will you tell me?"

He'd arrived in the city with $2,000 and taken the furnished room at the George Washington. At night, he'd go to a club called the Bar Point. In the front room were backgammon, gin rummy, and chess; in the back room was an illegal poker game. Howard was relatively unfamiliar with poker, and since he had what seemed to him at the time like a substantial wad of bills, he decided to learn how to play. The game was strictly two-bit, but Howard was so terrible that he lost nearly all his money within two weeks. He decided to pay ahead on his room before playing again.

The next day, he'd gotten into line at the front desk to pay rent. A shirtless man rushed up to him, yanked the money from his hand, and absconded. Howard didn't know what to do and he was too proud to ask my parents for help. A week later, his possessions were confiscated by the hotel management. He was out on the street.

He slept in the park during the day and hung out at the Bar Point at night. To make money, he ran errands for the players. They wanted sandwiches and cigarettes and he'd fetch them at the Korean deli across the street. By midnight he'd have ten or twenty dollars, enough to sit down in the game. He played every hand then. The seven-two off-suits, the threes with a king and a queen on the board. He was a believer in luck then, luck, which resembles nothing more than a mangled version of hope.

Some nights the cards would run cold, and he'd lose his money quickly. In the morning he'd lie in the sun, on the cool tufted grass, and think back on the night before, going over the hands in his mind until he figured out what he'd done wrong. Sometimes he would have done nothing wrong, would have been a casualty of fortune, plain and simple. Other times he'd see that he could have done things differently, that if he'd played the numbers right he'd have come out ahead.

He fell in love with the game of poker—not just with the cards, but with the money and the banter and the drugs. He loved the way the last card came, the surprise of it, the exhilaration that coursed through his body when he took a pot. They came only three, maybe four times an hour, but when they did, he'd pull the chips in with the enthusiasm of a child presented with a new toy.

Before his relations with our parents had soured to the point of his leaving, his plan had been to move to New York and, in the fall, begin his freshman year at Columbia University, where he'd been accepted the previous spring. Howard became so enmeshed in the world of underground gambling, however, that he scrapped his original plan, a decision that worried and angered our father, who had lost any power he may once have had to convince him he was making a mistake.

One day the Bar Point's owner, a small reptilian man named Goichburg, had to shut the club down for a trip he was taking to Philly. Howard offered to clean the club spotless in exchange for a place to sleep, and Goichburg agreed. He spent the weekend mopping and dusting. He ran rags along the windowsills, even cleaned out the toilets. When Goichburg returned, he was so impressed with Howard's work that he kept him on. During the long afternoons, Howard slept on the couch, and at night he would play in the game.

After some months, Goichburg appointed Howard to manage the table. Howard would take a small rake, or fee, from the players and he and Goichburg would split the profits. Even in this proprietary role, Howard would play through the weekend, sitting for seventy hours straight, mesmerized by the endless permutations of the deck. He would lower the rake to keep the game going. The players snorted buckets of coke and by Sunday afternoon they'd be out of their minds, their vision too blurry to read the cards properly. Flushes would be shown that weren't flushes, pairs would be brandished, then retracted. That diamond was a heart. That ace was a four. "You're crazy, you know that," Howard would say. "You want an egg sandwich?" And the player in question would stay in the game against whatever better judgment he had.

One of the players was a softspoken cokehead named Mitch—the same Mitch who'd come up with Howard for the Dart—and the two of them became fast friends. After living in the club through the summer, Howard moved into Mitch's one-bedroom on Grand Street and slept on the living room couch.

In order to fund his bad habits, Mitch rented the bedroom to a middle-aged man with a paunch, a gay waiter named Joe. Joe liked to comb the gay clubs and pick up teenage boys from New Jersey. They were pimply and confused, wearing stiff leather jackets and chains on their wrists. Some days Howard would wake up in the choked light of morning to see Joe, the gay waiter, kissing some kid on his thick pouty mouth.

The apartment was stifling. The windows wouldn't open. Mitch kept seven mangy cats and rarely changed the litter. There was cat shit everywhere, in the bathroom and the corners. The dishes sat in the sink. The sink dripped. The faucets in the bathroom dripped. The toilet ran, and because the apartment was so wretchedly unkempt, so utterly unpresentable, Mitch refused to call a plumber. The landlord didn't care. The landlord didn't know. Howard, who had never been especially neat, was disgusted enough to take out the garbage, but for the most part he ignored the filth. His life was at the club. His bed was in the apartment, and as long as he had to pay only $150 a month to sleep there, he wouldn't sleep anywhere else.

After some months of living with Howard and Mitch, Joe, who was paranoid to begin with, had a breakdown. He waited one day in the dark of the apartment with a long, shiny knife. Howard walked in the door and there, in the gloaming, with a knife in his hand and just underwear on, was Joe.

"You don't need to kill me," Howard said. "We can talk about this."

The two of them sat in the apartment for hours. Howard was afraid that Joe would kill him, and Joe was afraid that, if he let go of the knife, Howard would turn it on him. After hours of making the most patient assurances, Howard convinced Joe that it was in no one's interest to commit a murder. "Look," he said. "I'll keep my hands up in the air, like this. You just run out the door and I promise not to follow you." Joe dropped the knife, put on extra pairs of undershorts, and fled out into winter.

I tell you Howard's story as if it were scary and terrible, which I imagine it was at the time. He, on the other hand, tells it with relish. He explains that there's a poker hand called the Gay Waiter (a number of hands have garnered nicknames through the years). "Queens full of treys," he chuckles. "You know you're in trouble at the end of a hand when your opponent informs you he's got the Gay Waiter."

5 ♠ Old Money

I had never understood the designation. It had surrounded me, like the plush of a chair, ever since I'd been born, but I didn't know what it was. As a little girl I'd imagined rotting, stinking piles of cash. Old in the way that compost is old. Hoarded, recycled, reused. It was a thing you couldn't eat, a thing you couldn't share. It was meaningless to me, except insofar as the possession of it separated my family from the families who'd attended St. Paul's for generations.

As I got older, I was able to discern the subtleties. Those who had it would summer in Maine or Southampton. Those who didn't, like us, would stay put. Those who had it would return to the school after Christmas with glowing golden tans. Those who didn't stayed pale. Most of all, those who had it played it down. The older the money, the more invisible it was; the newer, the more flaunted.

Though I wasn't especially envious of the other students' money when I enrolled as a third-former (the British designation for a ninth-grader) at St. Paul's in 1986, I was covetous of their social rituals. I learned soon enough that they all went to the same Hamptons beach club and that their women debuted at the Waldorf-Astoria. All of them attended dancing school together, as I discovered one night in a breezy, humid hall during the yearly semiformal when I couldn't manage a foxtrot to save my life. Whether the other students liked their worlds or not, they knew just how to act. Their environments were familiar to them as the palms of their hands, and I imagined the immensity of their tradition was like a cool gust of wind at their backs, floating them through lives of happy leisure.

One of the girls I met at the school was a scion of a very old, very rich family and had a habit with money that thrilled me. Her name was Aurielle, and her face was pale and pointy. She looked like a very friendly dog, but when she cried, which she did rather often, her face would dissolve into the picture of a brokenhearted heroine. Her overbearing mother made her keep assiduous track of her expenses, down to the penny, and at the end of each month, she was expected to fill out a financial statement, complete with a line for "sundries and miscellaneous," to send to the family accountant. One dreary, overcast afternoon, I stepped into Aurielle's ground-floor room and watched her type up her report. When I asked her why her mother would make her do such a thing, she looked at me and shrugged. "It's practice for when I get older," she said, as if it were the most natural thing in the world for a ninth-grader to be typing up an expense report. "You know, I have to give ten percent of my allowance to charity," she added, as if to apologize.

Until I matriculated as a student at the school, where I

could see up close the marvelous accoutrements of wealth, I hadn't realized how truly middle-class my family was. There was a part of me that denied this fact vociferously. Even though I'd seen very few specimens to match the description, I believed that only the most stereotypical Americans qualified as middle-class. My father was the son of Jewish immigrants, and my mother was an actress. My brother, I had recently discovered, was a hard-bitten gambler in New York, and my sister, at least as I perceived her then, was preternaturally vicious—exacting my torture with elegance and grace. The members of my family were simply too *interesting* to be anything as plain as middle-class.

I remember the first weekend that school was in session. Three years earlier, my mother had gone to rehab to stop drinking, and after two years of living absently and soberly in the house, she'd decided she needed to leave for New York to pursue her lifelong dream of becoming an actress. The doctors had told her that if she wanted to get better, she needed to follow her dreams, and my father and I had at least partially resigned ourselves to the fact that the doctors knew best. Aside from the fact that she looked and smelled so different—seemed a stranger—the afternoon was a remarkably pleasant one. My mother loved to shop, and she welcomed the opportunity to spend money on items that I truly needed. Every time we picked out an article of clothing, she would take it in her hands, fold it, and give it a little pat.

"This is *extremely* preppy," she would say. "You'll fit right in." I was relieved by these pronouncements. I trusted my mother to know what was required for me to pass with the other students. We drove back to the campus with a carload of furniture, toiletries, and clothes. I was especially excited about a red canvas chair that folded out "to make room if you need it for visitors," and a green braided rug that my mother declared "*very* tasteful."

· · ·

I spent most of my first year asleep. The moment classes began, it was as if I'd been overtaken, like Dorothy, by the odor of poppies. In retrospect, I was suffering under the weight of a depression blacker than any I could have imagined for myself, though I didn't label it then. I simply believed that I was lazy, and I hated myself for it. I would lie in the narrow metal bed, unable to get up, drifting in and out of uncomfortable slumber. I'd regularly wake up terrified, having dreamed about my brother, with his roll of snapping bills, walking around in the dangerous city. But I never called him. An invisible barrier separated my two lives—the life I had at school and the life that I loved in New York—and I was eager to maintain it.

The room itself was synonymous with loneliness. The walls were bare white, their paint peeling away in leaflike swatches; the windows were opaque with weather and sunlight. I would sit in my red canvas chair, waiting for visitors I knew would never come, venturing out on occasion, if only to escape its isolating walls. I was logical enough to know that friends were not made by waiting around in the dank of a dorm room, but I couldn't seem to budge myself, let alone start up a conversation.

The red canvas chair glowered in the corner of the room. It was the specter of my mother. The rug, the clothes, even the toiletries, with their creamy, scented ointments and feminine designs—all of them reminded me of her.

I would wander the dormitory hallways like a wraith, listening in on conversations that I couldn't really hear, or sit on a faded blue armchair in the common room for hours, watching people come and go. One girl would sit out on the pocked, stone stoop, blowing bubbles, waiting like a siren for the boys to pass by. She was a debutante from New York, beautiful and graceful, but she seemed just as lonely as I, sighing softly to the air.

The dorm itself was one of four residential buildings in an area of campus called the Quad. They were handsome brick buildings, industrial and sturdy. Down the hill there was a shallow swamp that would swirl with ghostly mist in the mornings, and through which the students would tromp to get to class, their knapsacks like whorls on their backs. My sister had lived in the very same dorm I did during one of her years at the school, and my brother had lived in a boys' dorm called Manville, which was just across the walkway.

When I first arrived at the school as a student, I felt that it belonged to me. I had grown up there; my sister and brother had been students there; my father was a teacher there. I'd explored the vast network of interlocking walking paths when I was just a tiny child, and to hear the other students talking about their various explorations and discoveries—discoveries I'd made so many years before they had even arrived—offended me. As I learned the habits of the rich, however, I grew to realize that none of it belonged to me, had ever belonged to me. Like a mouse inhabiting the walls of a palace, I had foolishly believed that I could claim it as my own.

Laura was a pretty girl who lived just down the hallway from me that first year. She was the epitome of eastern Old Money, and I regarded her with a mixture of fear and curiosity. I'd read *The Preppy Handbook,* and I realized that Laura was the very same girl they'd diagrammed in that volume. She was blond, slightly taller than average, with powder blue eyes and a scarlet, bow-shaped mouth. She hailed from Maryland and was the niece of a prominent senator. She was wealthy beyond belief but never blatant with her money. She'd complain of her empty pocketbook, even as she grasped it with her dainty, burnished nails.

The entire dormitory was a nest of bulimics and anorectics, and those of us who escaped such afflictions were, if nothing else, chronic dieters. One of the things I admired most about Laura was that she was easy with her intake. She was obsessed with Cup O' Noodles, and kept a case of it under her bed. One day she wandered the halls, crying like a cat in heat, *"Cup O' Noodles, Cup O' Noodles."* Her supply had run out and she was famished. She knocked on my door, surely the only visitor I'd have that day, and asked me if I'd lend her a cup, but I didn't keep Cup O' Noodles in my room.

I often skipped dinner that year, afraid that I'd have to sit alone. By curfew I'd be hungry enough to brave the Community Center, a squat brick building that flanked one of the campus ponds, and buy some Doritos. In the winter the pond would freeze over, and on bright days the students would pour over the esplanade to ice-skate. I'd look on at such scenes, dumbfounded by the innocence of them, and dream about my next trip to New York.

For Lent, Laura gave up her beloved Cup O' Noodles. "It's making me balloon," she cried. "And I don't want Tommy to break up with me. I don't know what I'd do."

"I thought that once you have a boyfriend you don't need to worry so much about your weight," I said.

"Oh, you have it backwards, my dear," she replied. "That's

when you *really* have to worry. You can't cover up! They feel everything with their little eager hands!"

Tommy was a sixth-former at the school, and he wasn't bad looking. He had magnificent blue eyes and a deep golden tan. Laura's comments shocked my imagination into picturing Tommy's spindly fingers searching Laura's belly for any hidden flab. The thought troubled me. There was something in Tommy's features that I didn't fully trust—a proximity of the eyes, a thinness to the lips—and I believed he would do Laura wrong. The fact that Laura was so adorably naive, in no small part because she had nothing to hide and everything to expose, made me even more suspicious of Tommy. I would wait, half coiled, on my tiny single bed, listening from across the hall for trouble.

One day, for reasons that I didn't fully understand at the time, Laura and Tommy invited me across the hall for some pizza. I was so unused to socializing, let alone to accepting such a proper invitation, that I found myself unable to do anything but stammer.

"You do like pizza, don't you?" Laura said, placing her hand on my shoulder.

I nodded yes, frightened by the very perfection of her face and bones. "I, I . . . I *love* pizza."

"Wonderful, wonderful," she said. "Come and have some pizza then."

Upon entering Laura's room, I relaxed—for that's precisely what the room was meant to make a person do. The bed, which, like mine, was small and lumpy underneath, was decked out in comforter after comforter, each covered in some warm-colored, French floral pattern. There was an eyelet lace dust ruffle, pillows galore, and a ragged old teddy bear, presumably the creature with whom Laura slept as a child. This careful ensemble had the effect of making the bed seem twice as large and a million times as luxurious as it was, and I couldn't help but to imagine Tommy closing the door behind him, tumbling onto the bed, and brandishing his little eager hand. (I almost imagined it gloved, as if to test for dust.) This image had me asking myself how Laura could be noshing on pizza in front of him, but I then realized she wasn't really eating the pizza at all, merely nibbling. With this observation, I sat down in the corner, picked a steaming slice of pizza from the box, and started feasting.

"Is it good?" Laura said, settling like a kerchief on her bed.

"Great," I replied, a glob of tomato sauce dribbling down my chin.

Tommy, who was sitting next to Laura, began the assessment. "So how do you like it here so far?" he asked.

"It's OK," I said. "I like it better than living at home."

"It must be strange for you to come here—your father being a teacher and all."

"I guess," I said. "But there are other faculty children here, so I don't feel too out of place."

"Right," Tommy said. "I know George, Mr. Taylor's son—a *genius* lacrosse player, that guy."

"Have some more pizza," Laura said, peeling a slice from the box. "You must be *starving.*"

"So we hear your brother's a gambler," said Tommy, feigning nonchalance.

"And that your mother's an actress," Laura added, leaning forward, her small freckled nose wrinkling up, as if it were the most adorable thing in the world for my mother to be an actress.

I stopped chewing for a moment, tempted to spit out the pizza and leave the room. Whether or not I might have been embarrassed or ashamed of my mother and brother was beside the point; Tommy and Laura had taken it upon themselves to be embarrassed for me.

"Yes," I said, making my eyes comically wide. "My brother's a world-class poker player. He's very rich!"

"And he gambles on sports, too," Tommy asked.

"Yes, I think so, though I've never really asked him much."

"And he lives in New York?"

"Yes."

"Is gambling legal there?"

"I think so."

"But you don't know."

"Well . . ."

"I hope you don't mind us asking you these questions," Laura said, her voice soothing. "You just seem kind of lonely over there across the hall is all."

I wasn't then wise enough to see the connection between my loneliness and my brother's gambling, but Laura apparently was.

"And your mother and father," Tommy blurted out. "Do they know your brother's a gambler?"

"Yes," I said, eager to get the interrogation over with. "It's not a big deal. It's probably like your dad if he's a banker. Working with numbers and all."

"Oh, no," retorted Tommy. "It couldn't be anything like my dad. My dad works at Morgan Stanley. And besides that, we're not Jewish." At this, I decided that, no matter how much I liked his peppy girlfriend, Tommy was truly repugnant, so I left.

6 ♠ New Money

I would never have expected my father to have remained in New Hampshire once the family had dispersed, but he did, for several years. In the city of Concord, the median temperature, including stifling summer days, is 39 degrees, and it's usually well beyond April before the winter cold subsides. My father hated the freezing weather, and I can vividly recall the sound of his curses as he'd scrape the night's accumulation of ice off the windshield. I'd jump out of bed and pull on some pants, then bolt out the door and try to calm him. On especially bad days I'd get in the car and turn on the ignition in the hopes that the heat from the engine would loosen the ice.

"You're gonna give yourself a heart attack," I'd say.

In spite of the relentlessness of the cold, year in and year out, and in contrast to the students at the private school, who'd be off to warmer climes whenever the opportunity would present itself, my family had hardly ever left the state, let alone the chill Northeast. The one vacation that I'm able to remember I recall only dimly. I must have been six, maybe seven, years old. The five of us had flown in a cramped DC-10 down to Disney World, where tropical storms had poured rain on our slackening bodies. My mother insists that I just don't remember the good times, and that I sang for the duration of the trip:

It must be a mighty big convoy
Rocking through the night

I tell her that, no matter how hard I try, I can't recall the singing, nor can I conjure up the image of the figurines—Snow White, Sleeping Beauty—that she bought me at the gift shop. The one thing I'm able to recollect in any detail is the all-you-can-eat Swedish smorgasbord. Though I don't know why we would ever have chosen to eat there (the food was soft and greasy on the eyes), I do know that Howard piled his plate high with giant meatballs and bratwurst, devoured every atom, then proceeded to vomit on the laps of nearby diners.

In the end, I suppose we simply hadn't had the money to take many real vacations, and we'd probably lacked the necessary wherewithal as well. Whatever the reasons, they no longer applied once the family disbanded, and my father decided the two of us needed a sunny few weeks. "We're off to Jamaica for winter vacation," he announced one cool afternoon in late autumn. And though I knew even then, as a sophomore at St. Paul's, that Jamaica wasn't any St. Bart's, I was thrilled.

Once we got off the plane, a small white van greeted us at the airstrip, and we ended up sharing it with two stringy women who, like us, had boarded in Boston and transferred at Fort Lauderdale. They looked about forty, with frazzled, husklike hair, and neckfuls of primitive jewelry that bespoke extensive experience traveling in tropical climes.

"You'll love Negrille," said the one on the right, her eyes rolling wildly in their sockets. "A real *native* hangout. Nothing to do but lounge on the beach and smoke ganja!" The other woman, who, like the first, was outfitted in a flimsy, cotton dress and battered espadrilles, snickered and threw me a look. I had, as had most of my friends, tried pot back at home, but I had in no way planned on smoking ganja on this rarest of all things—a vacation with my father. Rather, I supposed I would spend all my days at the beach, catching up with him on the latest in English grammar and soaking up the rays so that I might sport a tan, however cheaply gotten, upon returning to St. Paul's.

The hotel was something else, a white stucco number, neither snobbish nor exclusive. Upon arriving at the front desk, I'd immediately noticed a throng of sweating natives swarming the beach, offering the tourists their cheap, homegrown pot. As it happened, I was eager to observe the Rastafarian culture at closer range. Our aunt Mary, my mother's half sister, had spent some years living as a Rasta in the Jamaican bush. Her complexion was deathly pale and her hair was flaming red—she was apparently the exclusive repository of all the Irish genes that my mother's rather mongrel side of the family could lay claim to. When I was young, Aunt Mary had visited once or twice, and I can vividly recall her bright red dreadlocks, which she'd stuff into a multicolored macramé hat. By the time my father and I unpacked our belongings and headed toward the beach, I'd already thought of any number of ways to ask the sweaty-chested vendors if they'd heard of a woman named Mary, who hailed from the well-to-do state of Connecticut.

At breakfast the next day, I was surprised by my father's composure. Whether it was the pleasant warm weather or the salty ocean air that was slathering itself on our bodies and faces, he seemed more happy and relaxed than I'd ever seen him. He ordered two fried eggs, sunny-side up, and a tall glass of pineapple juice, which, when it arrived, he proceeded to guzzle with the alacrity of a man who's been lost in the desert for years.

"I was thinking we'd swim a little, take in the town, and then nap?" he asked. "I need to do a little reading, but other than that I'm all yours." I looked up at my father, his face a faded yellow from his years of artificial sun, and smiled.

"You do all the work you want," I said. "All I want to do is get a tan."

"You do love the sun, don't you?" he exclaimed, impressed by my sturdy resolve. "Well, go get your suit on and let's lie out, goddammit!"

When I came out of my hotel room, wearing the only bathing suit I had, I realized I'd made a horrendous mistake. The suit, which was white with giant pink and purple flowers, was too tight at the crotch and shoulders, so I had to hunch over in order to walk. This hunching had the effect of making me look like an Igor, and as I waddled toward the beach chairs, where my father was already baking, the suit began to creep between my buttocks. By the time I lay down, I had the most terrific wedgie of all time.

"We'll have to get you a new suit," my father remarked. "Maybe when we go into town this afternoon." Until then, I decided I would go about getting a tan in the most scientific way possible. I would lie in the sun for forty-five minutes to an hour, spending half of that time on my stomach and the other half flat on my back, then allow myself to swim in the ocean for a brief interval in order to cool off. I'd already donned my tortoiseshell sunglasses, which I adored not only because they reminded me of that most glorious afternoon I'd spent shopping with my brother, but also because my horrifically pale, veiny skin looked almost tanned when viewed through their soft greenish lenses.

Once we got into town, which was composed primarily of one main street that snaked its way around broken-down shacks and leaking fire hydrants and jumped a small, rushing river before transforming itself rather clumsily into a rundown, potholed highway—the highway we'd driven with the two stringy women—we stood for a moment on a corner and waited. There was a slight altercation in the street between two enormous Rastas, and I remember putting my glasses in my pocket in an attempt to remain inconspicuous.

After the fight had dispersed, my father and I proceeded down a small, grassy slope, at the bottom of which sprawled an open-air market. As we wandered around, looking at the local wares, I bought some Bob Marley T-shirts and bootleg reggae tapes. When we finally arrived at a booth that sold bathing suits, I found myself having to choose between an ugly one-piece with an elephant print and a minuscule bikini embossed with the faces of Gandhi and Martin Luther King. Though I realized I'd get a fuller tan if I purchased the bikini, the thought of wearing the legends of the struggle for civil liberties all over my bottom and breasts made me wince.

"You choose whichever you want," my father said, handing me more than enough money to pay. Even though I knew he was no longer broke (not only were there fewer mouths to feed, but he'd had some recent success writing columns about English for the local city paper), I was taken aback by his generosity.

My father had always worked hard, but in the year or two previous to our trip to Jamaica, he'd stepped up his routine. Ever since my mother had left him, his habit had been to emerge from his bedroom at seven in the morning, still in his pajamas, and proceed to the kitchen, where he'd devour several Hostess chocolate doughnuts while leaning indelicately over the sink. My father had such a ravenous sweet tooth that the dreary little kitchen would seem to brighten with his appetite, and I'd covet those moments when I'd catch him in the act of eating breakfast. Once he'd finished with the doughnuts, he would make his way to the study, where he'd pound hunt-and-peck style on his baby blue Remington, muttering from time to time, rubbing his thighs with his palms. Sweat would stream down his chest and back; it would pool in his belly button, then melt down his legs till his pants were soaked through. The sound of clackety-clacking would be so ubiquitous and maniacal that I'd half expect to see ALL WORK AND NO PLAY MAKES JACK A DULL BOY typed over and over again on a million loose-leaf sheets that he'd hidden in a drawer. It didn't seem possible that one man could unleash so much writing on the world.

As a teacher at the school, my father had always been considered a great eccentric, and his physical presence only added to his charm (his nickname was Jumbo Shrimp, both because it was an oxymoron and because he just loved shrimp). His Jewishness set him apart from the start, however, and several members of the faculty regarded him as strange. He loved to tell me a story about one of his first years at the school. They'd asked him to read from the Torah at chapel, and he'd readily agreed. He'd practiced for his big debut in the afternoons, reading through the Hebrew, just the rudiments of which he understood. In his edition of the holy text, the consonants were printed in boldface, while the vowels appeared only faintly underneath. When the time finally came for him to ascend the pulpit, he faltered. The candlelight was flickering, the night outside was moonless dark, and he couldn't see the letters properly. He decided to just make it up as he went along, and for nearly ten minutes, he recited pure gibberish to the faculty and student bodies of that venerable institution. He feared he'd be a laughingstock, if not outright fired, but much to his relief, when the service had finally come to an end, both students and teachers approached him, extended their hands with the deepest admiration, and told him what a beautiful text it was that "his people" had written.

Though it certainly sounds a cliché—the stiff if magnanimous father who loves to tell jokes—my father was beyond mere epitome; he was the archetype embodied. Though it looked to most casual observers as if my father were a real literary type, actual stories were not his primary interest. Like those doctors who eschew the flesh of the living in favor of the study of the skeletal dead, my father was fascinated by the fundaments of language. He would pick it apart and put it back together again. His puns would walk around like little Frankensteins, impressively compact but frightening. To speak with my father was like playing a game of Jumble Word, and this could be daunting. I quickly learned the rules for using "lie" and "lay" and marveled at the fact that my feet could smell and my nose could run. My father fancied himself, in various incarnations, Attila the Pun, and Conan the Grammarian, and in 1990, a couple of years after our trip to Jamaica, he was named International Punster of the Year, an award bestowed upon him by the International Save the Pun Foundation. By that time, he'd published a book called *Anguished English,* which went on to become a national best-seller, thereby relieving him both of his chronic worries over money and, later, once he'd written several more books, of his duties as a teacher at the school.

• • •

After our long day of shopping for bikinis and lying supine on the beach, my father and I went to a bar. It was basically a hut that had been set up on the oceanfront so that singles could mingle, their skin still aglow from the tropical ablutions of the day. As I sat at the bar, sipping gingerly from my virgin strawberry daiquiri, I could feel my shoulders burning with sun and my nose glowing red in the moonlight. I do not think I had ever been happier than I was at that moment, and I started to cry. My father put his hand on my back and looked at me with worry.

"Are you having a breakdown?" he asked. I told him I wasn't, that I was just happy to be there after a long day of sun. Whatever jumbled sentence I produced in order to communicate this sentiment must have alarmed him even more, for he immediately paid the bill and led me across the unlit beach to our hotel, which was fifteen minutes away by foot. While the bar had been populated almost exclusively by white tourists, the beach was a hangout for partying locals and as we walked, rather briskly at first, then slowing down as we neared the beaming lights of our hotel, local after local approached us, trying to sell us their ganja and trinkets.

Once we got to the hotel, and before we went up to our rooms, I realized I'd misplaced my tortoiseshell sunglasses. I searched my pockets—nothing. I then looked through my father's leather bag. They were not there. I ran up the stairs to my room, which was clean and brightly lit, its ceiling fan whirring in the cool evening air, and ransacked every nook.

"My glasses are gone," I shrieked, bolting down the stairs past my father. "I have to go back to the bar!" I knew that I'd probably lost them while lying on the beach that afternoon, and so, against my father's wishes, I headed out the door. I walked toward the ocean and bent over, imagining that the glasses might have washed up on the shore. When I realized they'd never show up there, I started running toward the bar.

"Where are you going!?" my father yelled from the doorway of the hotel.

"I lost the glasses!" I yelled back. "Don't you understand? I need to find them." As I began to jog and then sprint back to the bar, my father started pounding his feet on the sand.

"Come back!" he demanded. *"Forget about the glasses. It's not safe!"* But I couldn't forget the green glasses. What would I say to my brother when I saw him next? And so I ran, past the bonfires and loitering drunks, until I finally reached the bar. Once there, I searched frantically, scouring the brown rattan chairs, skimming my hands over damp, plastic tables. The glasses were nowhere to be found. As I stood there, a thick-chested Rasta approached me.

"You are sad," he said, putting his hand on my shoulder. "Come sit dere with me and we talk it over." I went with him, not knowing what else I could do, and the two of us sat on a bale of sweet-smelling hay in the middle of the beach in Negrille.

"My name is Chris," he told me. He was smiling, his perfect teeth glinting in the light. He pulled a pack of American cigarettes from his pocket. "You smoke and den you tell me what happen."

I grasped the cigarette and saw my hand was shaking. "I don't know," I said, bursting into tears. "It's my father. He—"

"Where you fader?" said Chris.

"He's back at the hotel," I said, blubbering. "And I can't find my glasses and my brother bought them for me and he lives in New York and I think he's not safe. . . ." Chris nodded. "And I think he's very smart, but not so bright, and he bought me these glasses." I threw up my hands. "I feel like such a dork, losing things all the time, not being able to hold on to just one thing. . . ."

Chris kept nodding and flashing his beautiful teeth. "Well, we look for your glasses, den," he said, standing up and making as if to search the immediate premises. "I have de mushrooms at home," he went on. (I was so taken off guard by this statement that I didn't register it until days later.) "We have de mushrooms in de garden and we have de breakfast too. De fresh eggs from de hens. Tomorrow how 'bout you come over an' a we shroom?"

I was about to say something—something like "no"—but I heard someone yelling. It was my father. "Katy, Katy!" He'd cupped his hands around his mouth. His voice was really loud.

"I have to go," I said to Chris, stubbing the cigarette out in the sand. "That's my father."

Chris stared out at the lapping waves. "Dat dere is your fader, the tall crazy man?"

"Katy, Katy!" my father bellowed. "Katy!"

"I should go and tell him I'm OK."

"Yes, you go and do dat," said Chris (probably realizing I wouldn't be much fun to shroom with anyway). "But you come back here if you need de talk, OK?"

"OK," I said, running down the beach toward my father.

Once I returned to school after what seemed, at least to me, like a rather eventful vacation, I spent the first day wandering the hallways, jutting my face out defiantly, hoping other students would take note of my new golden tan. Whether or not my recent acquisition was ever even noticed, it was lost, like the glasses, abruptly. On the morning of my second day back, the skin on my nose started peeling, followed by the skin on my cheeks and my chin. By the end of my third day back, the tan had nearly disappeared, and all that remained were some swatches of sickly gray, which I picked at with my nails until they fluttered to the ground.

In the week following, my vanity was further bruised when a distant friend named Tim approached me in the School House Reading Room. I was sitting in a giant red leather chair when he came up behind me, clutching a copy of *Newsday* in his hand.

"Have you seen this?"

"Seen what?"

The raid on my brother's betting office had occurred during the Super Bowl. The Redskins and the Broncos had been playing for the championship when the police raided seven offices, confiscating $5 million in wagers. At the end of the article there was a paragraph listing the names of those who'd been arrested, and there, between Kevin Drury and Frank Evans, was my brother: "Howard Lederer. Age: 24."

"Maybe you should call your parents," Tim said, growing sympathetic. I wasn't sure whether I should laugh or cry. While my brother was being handcuffed and, I imagined, treated roughly by the cops, I'd been fretting over the loss of my cheaply gotten tan. I walked down the stairs toward the dormitory pay phone, breathing in the stale, institutional air, thinking my brother was going to jail.

7 ♠ The Figures

But I've yet to explain what it was that my brother was doing that would land him in jail in the first place. From the outside Howard looked like a bookie, and in New York this was a felony, but he wasn't a bookie. When he was younger, maybe twenty years old, he'd worked as a clerk for a bookie, but he'd quit after meeting his partner, Steve Z.

Z, whose real name was Stephen, after Stephen Daedalus, the character from the James Joyce novels *A Portrait of the Artist as a Young Man* and *Ulysses*, was Jewish and bald with a Fu Manchu mustache and a pair of ultragibbous eyes. His writer-editor parents had all his life primed him to become some sort of an artist, and when Z entered high school they'd enrolled him in afternoon acting classes in Manhattan, just down the river from Hastings-on-Hudson, where they lived. Z had liked acting, but he'd also liked gambling (a habit he picked up from his father, who played gin), and whenever he could find an out, he'd sneak over to a Forty-second Street club called the Flea House, where cigar-sucking Jewish men would gamble through the hazy afternoons. After dropping out of Columbia to act, he turned to gambling to support himself. He then returned to school—this time NYU—to study finance and statistics, a degree that helped him land a job at Harper & Row, where he worked for eight years before becoming a professional sports bettor.

By the time that Howard met him, Z had gained a reputation as the winningest independent sports bettor in the east, a vocation that, though not looked upon gladly by the authorities, wasn't technically illegal. Z made his living betting sports, but he wasn't a bookie. While a bookie takes a vig (short for "vigorish"), which is basically a commission on a given client's bet (in order to bet $100 on the Raiders to win, for example, a client will actually have to put up $110; if he loses, the bookie gets to keep the extra 10 percent), a bettor just takes a position. While the bookie will make money as long as the action on both sides of his line is the same, the bettor needs to pick a side and put his money down. Though the bettor takes the risk that he might lose on any given day, there's a greater potential for profit if he's good.

Z did so well that the moment his office placed a bet, the official line, or point spread, would change from New York all the way to Las Vegas. It took me a long time to understand how this could be, but one day, after many explanations, it came clear. In the '70s and '80s, before the advent of the Internet, sports information was very difficult to come by. To be a top-notch odds-maker, you had to wake up early, read through all the local papers, as well as *The Sporting News*, the *Daily News*,

The New York Times, and anything else that might contain a box score or a weather forecast. You had to try to find informants from various teams—trainers, doctors, janitors, anyone who would have access to information about the players—and you had to pay them for their information. You had to research how the team had done in other years, which players had been traded, which players had been added, how the roster would be ordered, and so on and so forth. In other words, you had to do a great deal of work in order to fashion a profitable line. With help from his various expert partners, known as handicappers, Z had been betting for years, and because of his success in placing his bets, bookie operations around the country would eagerly wait for a call from the Wise Guys, as Z's office was then known, and move their lines accordingly.

In order to be sure that his action was placed before anyone shifted their line, Z employed a number of callers to place all his bets in simultaneous fashion. The presence of these callers made the office look suspiciously like a bookie office, and the police had trouble believing that anyone could make money without taking a vig, so Howard and Z hadn't been particularly surprised by the raid. They spent two nights in the city jail, explained their position to an assistant DA, who listened to their tapes and agreed they weren't technically bookies, and were released. Actually prosecuting a bookie operation (whether real or perceived) is very difficult; there are no official records, no weapons, no bloody remains. It was the custom back then for the City of New York Police Department to make regular sweeps of suspected operations in an effort to frighten them out of the business, but Z, who had a good lawyer, wasn't frightened, and after Howard and he got out of jail, they decided to move their operation to Vegas.

But I knew next to nothing of any of this at the time. All I knew was that Howard was a gambler, that he made a lot of money, that he'd take me out to dinner, buy me shoes. I didn't even think about the real nature of gambling, that for Howard to win someone else had to lose, and so I lived in a happy oblivion until the autumn of my senior year when I visited my mother's small apartment in New York.

When I went to New York on vacations from school, I'd take the Trailways buses that St. Paul's would rent out to bring students back home to the fanciest sections of Boston and Greenwich. There would usually be two of them, idling by the tiny campus post office, the exhaust from their engines furling out like gray flags. By my sixth-form year, I'd managed to make a few friends, and I'd sit with them at the very back of the bus, doing bad things like smoking or maybe drinking some vodka once the driver had turned off the lights.

Just getting to Connecticut would take several hours, and after that, I'd board a commuter train to Manhattan, then hail a yellow cab, which would take me to my mother in the Village. She lived in a walk-up on the corner of Perry and Hudson, just above a Hunan Pan and across from the White Horse, the tavern where the poet Dylan Thomas had famously drunk himself to death. There was neither doorman nor light, and it would take me some time to toe my way up the stairs, then down through the crooked, dank hallway. By the time I would finally arrive at my mother's, it would be at least midnight, and on this night in particular, the roads having been rather icy in Concord and the cabs having been rather scarce in the cold, I was later than usual.

"I'll make you some soup once I'm finished," she said.

"Are you doing a puzzle?" She was sitting in her bedroom at her desk.

"No, I'm doing today's figures for Howard and Z," she remarked. "Come look if you like."

I walked, bewildered, toward the far end of the room, tripping on the corner of the bed. The space itself was so small, and the ancient hardwood floors so thick with clutter, that it was hard to pick one's way around the place.

"Your numbers are so orderly," I stammered, standing right beside her.

"I did very well in penmanship when I was young, if that's what you mean," she replied.

In front of her, scribbled all over a regular piece of graph paper, was a column of names that I didn't recognize. Next to each was a corresponding figure. "Mr. Bill," "Flounder," "The Dog"—such designations were neither familiar nor auspicious from where I stood, but I didn't have the presence of mind at that hour to ask what all the names and figures meant.

By the time I woke up the next morning, my mother had gone to the betting office for the day, and I figured it was time to search her desk. Perusing her drawers seemed as good a way as any to get the answers I was looking for. I remember thinking, as I entered her room, that it looked like her room had at home. The bedsheets were rumpled and the closet door was open. Through it I could make out piles and piles of shoes—Enzo, Martinelli, Nine West—their toes collapsed and their ankle straps twisted. The wilted shoes made me feel unbearably nervous, and I turned back toward her desk, which stood stolidly at the far end of the room. Upon reaching it, I felt unsure, not because my mother would be angry if I looked through her drawers, but rather because I wasn't clear about what I was searching for. I knew there would be crosswords and most likely an old deck of cards. Other than that, the three little drawers promised mysteries to be revealed.

When I opened the drawers, I found even more clutter and mess. Pens and pencils commingled with less congenial objects like scissors and oxidized subway tokens. What looked like important documents (parking tickets, contracts, leases) were stuffed haphazardly into the various drawers so that, upon opening and closing them, I could hear a faint rumpling sound. I imagined this was a booby trap, my mother's protection against the police, who would surely be coming to take her to jail any minute. After rummaging thoroughly, however, I realized there was nothing remarkable, let alone incriminating, in those drawers. Whatever evidence I was trying to gather in order to support my increasing suspicions was not in that desk. The only objects of mention, which I'd known about the night before, were the sheaves and sheaves of figures, each one an announcement that, no matter how unkempt her drawers may have been, the woman who sat at that small teak desk had impeccable penmanship.

Realizing there would be nothing more for me to learn, at least not until my mother got home, I retreated into the living room. I sat down on a little brown love seat and clicked the TV on. To my left was a beautiful stone fireplace, the one redeeming aspect of what was otherwise a dismal place. I marveled at the objets d'art: Native American dolls and birds carved out of wood, which my mother had propped up on the mantelpiece, and which were now staring down at me—or so it appeared from their unfeeling eyes—with contempt.

I'd visited my mother a handful of times, and had grown

fond of the little crooked side streets that ran through the Village like tunnels for mice. I used to walk down them whenever I'd visit my mother at *The Village Voice*, where she'd worked as a classified-ad taker, and then, later as the classifieds manager of *Seven Days*, their now-defunct magazine startup, before taking the job on with Z. I can very vaguely remember arriving at her office on some drear, muggy morning, sitting at a table in the grayish main room. There were two other women in the office that day, both of them in dark gray suits with matching gold accessories. One of them had handed me a tattered old copy of *Seven Days* before telling me my mother would be out to meet me shortly.

When my mother finally returned to the house, she looked positively elated. "We had a *brilliant* day," she exclaimed, peeling off her shoes. "Over two hundred thousand dollars on football, which means I'll get a big bonus this year." She threw her pea coat on the rack and went into her room, where she sat at the desk. I remember thinking she was an awfully strange-looking woman—her hair styled so that it clung to the sides of her head in little black wings, her gingham shirt ironed and tucked into her jeans. If I hadn't known she was working for a betting operation, I would have thought she belonged at a junior high bake sale, she looked so neat and clean. "You know," she said, after figuring her bonus on the desktop calculator, "*you're* going to get a lot of Christmas presents this year."

I sat down on the bed, clearing some clothing and papers away. "How much is it going to be?"

"There's still a chance we might just lose it all back—but if things keep up . . . let me just say it'll be a lot."

"What do you mean 'lose it all back'?"

"Well," my mother said, looking suddenly unsure. "What do you know about sports betting anyway?"

"Not much, actually," I said.

My mother bent over, pulled some papers from a drawer, and put them gently on my lap.

"You see these?"

"Yes, I saw them last night. 'The figures.' "

"Right, it's just a list really, of how much we bet with each bookmaker, the result of each bet, the amount that we owe them or they owe us—you know, like a balance sheet. It's the same thing you'd find in a bank."

"Except for the fact that these people are named 'Mr. Bill,' right?"

"That's right," my mother said. "We call bookies, like Mr. Bill, and they give us the line on a game—today it was a football game. If we win, they owe us money; if we lose, we owe them money. It's as simple as that."

(I remember remarking privately to myself that it didn't seem simple in the least, but I didn't want to interrupt my mother's progress.)

"The first thing you do, of course," she continued, wagging her finger in the air, "is to get yourself an office."

"Is the office as big as this apartment?" I asked.

"No, not even this big. And I'll tell you, it can get very crowded in there with all the people Howard and Z have working for them. On the worst days, like Sundays when there are lots of games, there are five or six of us trying to place the bets before the lines change, and it can be very frantic in there. The place is really a mess—I try to clean it up"—at this, my mother lit up a Merit—"but it's hard.

"The one good thing is that we have to move offices every once in a while—you know, to avoid 'the heat' " (she made little quotation marks with her fingers), "which means we get to start out with a nice clean office. We just move the desks and move the chairs and we take all the food that we can carry, and that's it, nice new office!" She started jigging around the room, holding her cigarette with one hand, snapping her fingers with the other—it was clear that the prospect of a big New Year's bonus was streaming hectic through her veins.

"And you make a lot of money this way?" I asked, wondering how much it could possibly be.

"Yes," my mother said, stopping cold and looking serious. "The group makes a *great deal* of money, potentially millions if we keep doing well. Howard and Z have a handicapper helping them. He lives in Nebraska. He's a recluse and he likes it that Howard and Z take on all the risk. They split up the winnings with him."

"So why didn't *he* get put in jail a couple years ago?"

"Oh, you mean the bust? Because the police are lazy. They know that we exist. But they don't understand what we do."

It all seemed so empty, like air. I needed something solid with which to compare it. "*The Godfather,*" I finally said. "Is it like that? Are we a part of the Mafia now?"

"No," my mother said. "Don't be ridiculous." She went into the kitchen, got a Tab from the fridge. "*Of course* we're not part of the Mafia."

"But isn't it dangerous for you to be involved in this business?"

"I suppose it might be a little risky, but if I'd stayed at the *Voice*, I would never have landed the Roundabout role." (She'd had a small part in their production of *The Crucible,* starring *Family Ties* star Justine Bateman.) "And I'd have a lot less money. But I've got a lot of work to do, so let's get you to bed."

I felt anxious as I walked toward the pull-out my mother started busily preparing.

"Now don't you worry, Miss Kate," she whispered. "Always worrying, you are. And biting your nails."

She put her face up close to mine. I turned my face away.

"I see," she remarked, as she padded back into her room, where she'd work until three in the morning most nights. I would stare for many hours at the light that seeped under her door.

8 ♠ The Family Business

I couldn't understand why Annie had decided to schedule her wedding for the stinging month of February, or why she'd chosen to have it at our maternal grandmother's house in Darien, the most frigid and tight-lipped of Connecticut communities. Whatever the reasons, the event was going to make for a bona fide family reunion. Not since the morning, nearly ten years before, when Annie had gone to New York for the summer, had the family been together in one house.

The house itself was a quaint white Colonial with a well-tended lawn and immaculate kitchen. (I remember the way my grandmother would roll up a bag of potato chips and wrap it extra tightly with a brittle rubber band.) As children, my siblings and I had always loathed visits to the house. Our grandmother had objected to my mother marrying a Jew ("The kids will all have kinky brown hair," she'd warned), and whenever we'd walk in the door she'd cast a cold eye on our coifs and our schnozzes. She was a lifelong heavy drinker, but of a very different sort than my mother had been. To an unobservant eye, nothing about the woman—from her carefully ironed white shirts to her hair, which was bobbed and curled up at the ends—would have seemed out of place. She was a domineering presence, and unless one saw it for oneself, one would never have guessed that she kept a half gallon of Popov on her washer, and that whenever she passed by the laundry nook she would take a stiff swig before going on her way. She must have taken at least twenty of these swigs a day, but she seldom lost her composure.

My mother tells me now that I was with her in the car when she drove up for the wedding from New York, but I can't remember this. All I can remember—or the first thing I remember—is the tiny front room of the house. My uncle Michael, who was autistic, was folded over in a chair, watching as the wedding guests arrived. He was a jovial man, a little over forty, with the countenance and spirit of a twelve-year-old. Indeed, his emotional age was fixed by the autism, and though he was an idiot savant, able to tell you the exact definition of any word you asked of him (he used to tear through the dictionary and he loved both his Bible and his *Wonder Woman* books), and though he could beat almost anyone in checkers, he behaved like a child. His eyes were dark and impish, and whenever he spoke he would clench up his fists, stomp his feet, make a scene.

When I asked him if Annie was around, he exclaimed: "Oh yes! Oh yes! The Bride to Be! The Bride to Be is upstairs, but I want to play checkers!"

I told him I needed to go.

"But I want to play checkers," he insisted, bringing his face within inches of mine. "Will we be playing checkers later or not?" I told him I'd be happy to play with him later, but, for now, that I had to find Annie.

Even as I walked up the stairs to my grandmother's bedroom, I could hear the commotion. I knocked on the door.

"Who's there?" asked my mother.

"Just me," I replied.

When I stepped inside and closed the door, I saw a dim shape in the corner, a very slight girl in a matte pink Chantilly lace dress. It was Annie, in curlers, her hand to her lips. She was retching.

"I can't do this," she moaned. She was reeling around the room, a coral pink blur.

"Yes you can," said my mother.

"But I can't."

"Yes you can."

"What if I barf during the vows?"

"You won't barf," my mother said. "Just remember to breathe."

"But I can't, I can't breathe. . . ."

Looking at Annie's dress, it was hard to see there was a body beneath the gown, it was so loose. Her chest was sunken and her face was white. Because I was her maid of honor, I felt it was my duty to tell her how pretty she looked—that she made a perfect bride—but my tongue was all tied up. She *did* look pretty, but her prettiness was so entirely delicate that I feared a single word from me would shatter her already fissuring face.

Ever since her junior year at Columbia, Annie had been having the attacks. I remember hearing about them, but only vaguely, as if she were some crazy woman in the attic, her symptoms whispered over in corridors. I'd heard that she was losing weight, that she couldn't hold anything down, that she'd sometimes come home from her classes at school and cry and cry. I remember one visit she made to New Hampshire, just after our father quit teaching. We'd gone to a local seafood restaurant, just Annie, my father, and I, and she'd ordered everything in sight: a buttered baked potato, a lobster, some fries, a bowl of New England clam chowder, and a slice of chocolate cake. When the food arrived, Annie prodded and picked but she didn't take a single bite, and my father, who would normally have objected to such waste, simply lowered his eyes.

I'd spent my share of evenings at her tiny two-bedroom in Harlem. I remember the place had been tiny but clean, with no light. She had a cat named Amelia and another named Franklin, and these two would rub against my ankles and legs, attempting to get on my lap whenever I let my guard down. The couch was a futon, the table a chest. I suppose she was living as any college student would back then, but I marveled at her coolness. Whether or not I would mock her when she showed me how to dance or when she tried to paint my increasingly pimply face, I was secretly in love, and I would let my eyes wander over her body as she moved about. I wanted to take it all in: the stockings, the minis, the black plastic bangles, the heavy black liner around the eyes. I didn't fully comprehend the nature of her illness, and if she seemed a little thin, a little drawn around the mouth, then I figured it was hard to be a grown-up.

One of my favorite activities when I was young had been watching my sister put her face on. Every morning, she'd sit on the green and blue plaid couch, her knees tucked underneath her, and rummage through her cosmetics bag, which was full of sophisticated doodads. She would pat a bit of liquid foundation on her fingers and then smear it evenly over her skin. More often than not, you could see a sharp line just where the makeup ended and her neck began, but I'd keep this to myself and giggle through the day that everyone could see her little mask. After she'd applied her mascara and liner, I'd tease her and tell her she was a regular raccoon, in response to which she'd pummel me senseless, a beating I'd love. Nothing would thrill me more than the fear of her teenage body coming at me ham-handed and swinging. I would dodge the blows, imagining I was a mammal and she was a sad, clumsy dinosaur. "You are soon to be extinct," I'd boast, throwing myself to the floor and scurrying under the table, where she was too big to follow.

After graduating from college, she'd gone on to a Ph.D. program in psychology at the University of Pennsylvania, and it was there she'd met Bennie, the groom. Lanky and tall, he had a bunched-up, boyish face that exerted a remarkably calming influence over Annie. Whenever he was in the room, her entire body would relax, like a sail being let out over water, and it was she who had proposed.

• • •

Before arriving in Connecticut to be my sister's maid of honor, I'd been to only one other wedding before—at the age of five or six. The bride was the much older sister of my closest childhood friend, a girl named Margot, who had a densely freckled nose and sad blue eyes. She lived in a weathered gray house in the middle of town with her parents, both of whom taught music for a living. Ever since I'd known her, Margot's kindly gray-haired mother had been sick. Her kidneys had failed her, and three times a week she would have to be hooked up to a dialysis machine or else, as my mother would explain it, her blood would get "dirty" and "she'd die." In spite of her illness, she remained an active member of the local artistic community and would regularly play the piano for regional theater productions. She and my mother had met through such channels, and though I knew that Mrs. Anderson didn't altogether approve of my family (she was religious, a Christian, and sober as a chopping block), she forgave us enough to allow me to visit with Margot in the house, play piano, and devour all the pastries and cookies my stomach could handle.

The wedding had been held at a local church downtown (also named St. Paul's, like the chapel at school), and I remember sitting in the pews toward the back, horsing around. It was a big wedding, and I'd been relieved by the number of people in attendance, which meant that I could disappear. The thing I can remember best is the bride's white satin train, which undulated over her shoulders and back as she walked up the aisle. Even then, when I was young, I longed after faith, and the train seemed a symbol of this. My mother was a Christian, but she wasn't particularly religious. And while my father would take me to the local Unitarian church every Sunday, I hadn't been indoctrinated into any one religion, a fact that troubled me. I wanted very badly to believe in God, but I didn't have the slightest idea how to go about it.

One day I decided to become a member of the congregation at Margot's church. If I couldn't fit in back on campus, then I could fit in there, among the cheer parishioners who'd crowd into the church on Sunday mornings. I even joined the choir, an organization to which Margot had belonged for several years and of which she was a leader. I remember relishing the fact that I was clearly so close with a bona fide Christian—indeed, that I'd known her since the two of us were babies. She knew where all the uniforms were kept, all the candles, the place where they stashed all the wafers and wine, and I would follow her around, searching as hard as I could for my faith—in the closets, the cushions, beneath the dark pews. We would sing, then go back to her house and strum our acoustic guitars through the long afternoons. On some days, the two of us would hang out in the church and talk about ethics. I'd insist that if I ever got rich, I'd give all my money to charity. "I'll be a nun. The church will feed me and I'll send all my money to the starving babies in Africa," I'd say.

"You don't know what you're talking about," Margot would say, tearing bits of paper from a leftover flyer she'd found in her chair (she had a nervous and intractable paper-eating habit), putting them into her mouth, rolling them into tight balls. "You think these things now, but you'll change. Everyone changes. Everyone thinks that they'll give all their money to the starving babies in Africa, but they never do." She balanced a small piece of paper on her lip, tamped it down with the tip of her pointy pink tongue. "People like to keep their money."

I was startled by her cynicism. "Then what's religion for?"

She shrugged. "I've thought a lot about that question and I'm not really sure. I like to sing in the choir, and I like to listen to some of the sermons, but I don't know if I really believe in God. I mean, how am I supposed to know?"

"But you *have* to believe in God," I said. "You're a *Christian.*"

"So," she said. "It doesn't mean I have faith. Faith is something else. You either have it or you don't. I have faith I *might* have faith someday," she said. "But I don't have much faith now."

Later that morning we'd walked up the stairs toward the service. The assembled congregation was the usual: large men in parkas, their faces puffed up from the sharp winter wind, women with hair combs and tartans, their children as antic as they were sedate. The priest for the service, a small, wiry man with two earmufflike tufts on the sides of his head, had requested that the audience stand, that we sing from our hymnals. I looked around the room, at the members of the assembled congregation, all singing absently but dutifully along. I stared at my book, at the string of black letters that ran beneath the perfect staves. I tried to see the faith in them, but I couldn't seem to make myself.

In Shakespeare, a comedy invariably ends with a wedding, and I remember thinking, as my sister walked across the floor, her face drawn up perfectly, as white and well shaped as a doll's, that it had been, in spite of the drama I'd witnessed upstairs, a very funny, happy day. Bennie's brother, George, a plump, cherubic blond, had been hitting expertly on the wedding caterer throughout the afternoon; while his father, Pony, a rather outlawish character with a magnificent handlebar mustache, had marveled that his son would be marrying at all. My father, for his part, had held court all afternoon, standing gravely in a corner, his hands opening and closing like giant Chinese fans.

But then, as the wedding music began to play, he walked solemnly to the front of the room with Annie at his side. He was giving her away. When he got to the makeshift altar, he stepped to the left, allowing the groom to usurp his place at Annie's side, waving his hand back and forth, as if directing traffic. It had been a long five years, and perhaps he was glad to have someone else take care of his daughter; or perhaps he was thinking of some new contronym or palindrome, something for his latest book. No matter what it was, he must have known somewhere very deep inside, that he'd lost her, both to Bennie and Montana, where the two of them were moving.

I could feel my chest constricting in anticipation of the impending vows. When the minister asked the best man for the wedding band, he took it from his pocket then dropped it on the floor. I had been only to that one other wedding before, and so I thought that this must be part of the ritual—like the purposeful shattering of glasses against hearths or the pelting of the couple with rice. I suppose I remained unable to believe that some, if not most, things, that happen in life have no logical provenance or meaning—that most everything that happens is chance.

But then Bennie picked the ring up off the floor, pushed it onto Annie's bony finger, and promised to love her until death did them part.

9 ♠ Happiness

The first time I flew to Las Vegas, I came off the plane into a spacious and decidedly welcoming airport. It was McCarran, a clean, modern building that serviced the entire city, and I remember thinking, as I looked up at the happy ads, which were brightly festooned on the drab, metal walls, that I—my family—had finally found a better place. The air was auspicious, soft and sweet-smelling, and the people looked happy, their vacations stretched out tenderly in front of them like a $5.99 buffet.

Howard, who had moved to Las Vegas in large part to escape the harassment of the City of New York Police Department (my mother, who continued to do his numbers, had moved there as well), met me at the baggage claim, and I had no trouble picking him out from the crowd. He was as large as ever, even though he'd taken up the practice of veganism, a very strict form of vegetarianism that I'd discovered in my freshman year at college. Our father loved to exclaim that the two of us were real "Las Vegans" and then burst into sniggering laughter.

After taking my bag, Howard told me that a "whale," a very wealthy person who is terrible at poker, was in town and that he had to get back to the casino. Would I mind coming with him? No, not at all, I said. So I loaded my fake leather night bag into the trunk of his shiny new Lexus, and we drove.

Like anyone else, I'd seen pictures of casinos and I was fairly knowledgeable about the more famous among them, like the Sahara, Caesar's Palace, and the Dunes. Nothing, however, could have prepared me for the grandeur of the Strip. In its exaggerated colors and garish rococo one could glimpse the promise of outrageous fortune. Las Vegas: the most American of American cities—bright and cheap and all dolled up, like a drag queen—a city of hope!

As the two of us neared the Mirage, which from a distance appears to the eye as a gold-plated skyscraper, I found myself faceup against some eventual freedom, though I couldn't at that time have put it into words. It was, in all of its glittering particulars, the giddy antithesis of all my childhood mores. Approaching the Strip from the east side of town, my brother's Lexus purring and the great, winglike lights of the pink Flamingo Hilton flashing frantically above our heads, I felt glad, as if I had thrown off an especially suffocating caul.

Howard left his Lexus with the valet, and we approached the casino from the north end. As I entered, the air hit me first. It was a Brazilian-themed, sickly sweet, tropical admixture, heavy and succulent as mango. In the light of the Las Vegas strip, everything came suddenly into focus. I'd gone to one of the most wealthy and establishment high schools in the country, but no one there could speak about their money. It was hidden from view and avoided. For what purpose? What did the rich have to hide? I had all along assumed it was a courtesy, a form of politesse to the poor and middle classes, but as I stood in the middle of a row of glittering slots, I saw the wealthy in a different light. It was their own they were trying to protect—from the awareness that nothing in their world was any more sincere than what took place here; that their fussy high society was at base just an ornate hypocrisy. At least in Las Vegas you knew where you stood. The cons were cons, and the hookers were hookers. No one here took refuge in aristocratic fictions.

My brother kept asking me what I thought, how I liked it, and I beamed. Polished and proud, he was unafraid of anything. *I* was unafraid of anything. I stood at the brink of the casino floor, the lights and dings of the slot machines ringing gaudy in my ears, the cranks of roulette wheels spinning and spinning. It was the first time in my life that I didn't feel lied to.

The early '90s had seen a renaissance in Las Vegas poker. Steve Wynn, the fabled owner of Mirage Resorts, the high-end proprietor of Treasure Island, the Mirage, and later the Bellagio, had hired a man named Bobby Baldwin as his president. Bobby, a thin, stooping man with a squat, sanguine face, was a famed poker pro from the '70s and '80s. When Bobby got his hands on the reins at Mirage Resorts, he made sure that the poker action at his casinos would be some of the best in the world.

This wasn't an immediately intuitive decision. Poker, as many people do not know, is the only casino game at which a player can routinely win. Games like blackjack, roulette, and baccarat, not to mention unadulterated rip-offs like slots, are played against the house, and, in the long run, the house always wins. In poker, the players go up against other players, and the house takes a small rake, or fee, from the pot in order to make a profit. Most casinos can make much greater profit on a roomful of slot machines than on a roomful of poker tables, and so the majority of casino poker rooms are tiny and disheveled, just large enough to provide for authentic gambling color.

Bobby Baldwin's reasoning when it came to poker had partly to do with his past as a brilliant high-stakes player and partly to do with good business. He figured that if you hosted a fancy, high-stakes poker room, you'd attract those well-to-do tourists who hankered after poker. You wouldn't make a lot of money from their action at the poker tables, but on their way to their hotel rooms, they'd maybe drop a grand or two at baccarat or craps. The poker room at the Mirage was not all that different from a restaurant or spa; it was ancillary, like icing, an amenity for the mega-rich who wanted to play with the best in the world.

As two of the regular sharks, my brother and Z sat at their table and waited for suckers and whales. The stakes for Howard's typical game of Hold 'Em required that a player arrive at the table with a minimum buy-in of $20,000. He and Z shared the table with other professionals, some of whom had also moved to Vegas from New York. There was Erik Seidel, whom I'd met at the Mayfair; a pudgy, balding fellow named David, whom my brother and Z would later take on as a partner in their betting operation; and Mickey when he'd fly in from the East.

These were just the young ones, though. The real proprietors of the table were the gargantuan "Texas Dolly" Doyle Brunson and the debonair "Chip" David Reese. Doyle, a typical Texas cardsharp from Lubbock, was the grand poohbah of the poker world, the most famous player alive. His lips stretched from ear to ear in a severe, equatorial grimace so that, when he smiled, his face took on the aspect of a bogeyman. When younger, Doyle had been diagnosed with a tumor of the brain, and told that he'd die within months. Doyle hadn't died, however, and when they'd cut him open they'd found that the cancer had miraculously disappeared. Forever afterward Doyle liked to joke that he was living on borrowed time.

Just as much an archetypal poker pro, Chip was of a younger generation than Doyle. A graduate of Dartmouth, Chip was known for charming certain whales into playing him alone in a game of gin rummy. He'd lure the whale up to a hotel room, then squeeze him all night until his bankroll was gone. The other poker players, who'd have been slavering for the big action, would bitch and moan for days afterward that Chip had made off with the week's big catch. On some days, when my brother took me to the golf links at his country club, he'd wave his hand over at a palm-enshrouded mansion and mutter: "That's Chip's house. I'd like to have a house like that someday." It made me hopeful when my brother spoke of money in this way. It wasn't that I believed in the security of money, nor that I believed that having money made one happy—not really. Rather, I liked the very orderliness of greed. It was clear. There was nothing confusing about it.

• • •

One night, after watching my brother play poker, I drove to my mother's house, a spacious faux Tudor on the east side of town. There were a couple of cars in the driveway, one a Honda, the other an egg white Mercedes convertible. (Who was this woman? This woman with money?) I knocked and no one answered. I tried the door. It was unlocked and I went in.

"I'm here, Kate," my mother called.

"Where are you?"

"Right here, right here." I wandered in the dark, past the wide-screen TV, through the kitchen, which was open and large. My mother was sitting on an antique gold plush couch outside on the patio. She was wearing her nightie, had a cigarette cocked in her hand.

"I'm just finishing my book, wait a second," she said, flipping to the very last page. "Done! Now how are you?"

"Good, good," I replied, surveying the premises. Like all of the wealthy who lived in Las Vegas, my mother paid a gardening group to keep things looking neat and clean, to trim the thick grass and plant the bright flowers, to tend to the pansies, which were basking in moonlight. There was also a very large pool, which was flanked, just at the property wall, by a row of stately cypress.

"What do you think?"

"I like your trees."

"I had a hard time with that one, you see it?" She pointed to a crooked tree. "I tried to get Jorge to replant it, but he kept putting it a bit too far over, and then a bit too far the other way, and I just gave up. Now the neighbors can see into the house," she sighed. "I've done so much work, but there's so much more to do. I had the room upstairs papered and I ordered the carpets in the living room—did you notice them on your way in?—but they're too shaggy, not the right ones, and I have to return them. And the cats—the cats!" (My mother had always kept Siamese.) "They've gone completely ballistic. I don't think they know what to do with all this air!" She paused.

"Did you hear about Annie?"

"I don't think so," I said.

"That she's going to move here as well?" She'd been playing

in some game in a back room back in Montana to make her ends meet, but I'd had no idea that she'd gotten so serious about it.

"To Las Vegas?"

"Yes, to Vegas. Howard flew her down and observed her as she played. He decided she had talent and he offered to back her."

"To back her?"

"To put up all the money in return for half the profits." (This was, I later learned, a pretty typical arrangement, for a backer to offer to stake a new player or a player who was good at cards but terrible with money.) "I wish he'd back *me*," my mother went on. "Though I don't much like poker—but I'd like to be backed." My mother put her hand up to her chin and left it sitting there. "It might be nice to have Annie nearby, though you know she can be difficult. . . . But I've got to stop talking and get myself ready."

She was waiting for her personal trainer to call. His name was Dr. Beem. "They call him that because he used to ride bikes," she continued. "He got into a terrible wreck on his BMW motorcycle." He was tall and lithe, a muscular man with a sensitive face. "Howard told me about him. He's *very* good. You know, he makes me swim a mile every day. I never thought I'd complain about something like that, even if I've never been too much for working out, but that's a lot of swimming, if I do say so myself. I love to be out in the sun, though. I love the warmth. And then, if it's late, and I'm feeling up to it—maybe watching one of my shows, like *Homicide: Life on the Street*—I'll walk a few miles on the treadmill. When you visit, you can use it too. It's not a bad piece of equipment."

All the talk about exercise was making me hungry. "Do you have any food?" I asked, rubbing my stomach.

"Of course, you're hungry! I didn't even think. Have you had any buffet?"

I shook my head.

"Well, the fridge is over there," she said, pointing me to it. "There's another in the kitchen if you want something more." Howard had been paying her well. The entire office had been given generous bonuses that year. "I've got leftover veggies."

"OK, sounds good," I replied, opening the fridge, which was stacked with cans of Tab and bottled water.

"I've been thinking a lot," my mother went on. "Spending the entire morning out here and all, and I think I like Las Vegas. There's a theater company here and all those shows. Maybe I can start up with the acting again." She was slimmer than I'd seen her in a very long time, and happier. She had a blue pool and a well-appointed patio. She could spend her afternoons watching the sun set over cypress trees, in her nightie, in her very own backyard.

Maybe it had been only a matter of chemistry: maybe the family wouldn't have functioned well no matter where we had lived, but I couldn't help but associate my family's newfound happiness with the perky novelty and lavish materiality of Las Vegas. It was the polar opposite of the private school where we'd lived for so many years, and it struck me as wholly redemptive. It was, in my eyes, an effulgent, festive, kindly place, coddling the family and all its petty troubles in its intransigently cheerful atmosphere. Though it may sound crass or venal, I fell utterly in love with Las Vegas. I believed that it would save us, that together, as a family, we could play our little games and still be happy.

The first fact of the world is that it repeats itself.

—Robert Hass
from "One Body: Some Notes on Form"

10 ♠ A's

I know it's not much of a reason to choose a place to go to school, but the thing that attracted me to the University of California at Berkeley the most was its distance from the East. Across mountains and flatlands and desert moraines, it was very far away.

All my life, I'd been stared at, with pity and scorn, with occasional concern, and I hadn't particularly noticed. It was just how things had been for me. Reading *The Scarlet Letter* in college, I saw myself in the figure of little Pearl, my mother in the figure of Hester, an *A* emblazoned on her breast. My mother had been an alcoholic, and saying that word even now is very hard. The word itself is so therapeutic, so typical, and I never knew what was worse: that millions upon millions of families suffered just like mine, or that mine wasn't really so special.

I wouldn't want to make it sound as if the study of literature saved me, however, or that I achieved some sense of heightened understanding through my work. Though I read day and night, devouring all the books my professors assigned, even the ones they just mentioned in passing, I didn't do it in the name of intellectual passion; rather, I did it to satisfy a growing and implacable compulsion.

As a girl, I'd been a truly dismal student—the worst kind: apathetic, lazy. I'd regularly settled for C's, even D's, not caring in the least what might result from my indifference. Once I set foot on the campus of U.C. Berkeley, however, something mechanical started to tick deep inside, like a bomb, and I developed an obsession with grades. A's. They were gorgeous. Like bright metal rockets. A's were like money, and I worked harder for my A's than I ever had or ever will work at a real job. It was the first time, so far away from the members of my family, that I began to understand them, to understand the unappeasable nature of their compulsions. There was a deep inner satisfaction, as of an appetite, in getting A's, and all that literature, all those stories, they just passed me right by.

I had heard early on in my time as a student that the easiest A in the department was the poetry workshop. I don't know who from or when, but I suppose it was a generally known fact, and one day I found myself sitting in Café Bodega on the corner of Telegraph and Bancroft, just half a block away from campus. I would go to Bodega, get a mocha with soy, or a coffee, sit down at one of the marbleized tables, work a little, relish the air that flowed through the patio windows.

On this day, after getting my coffee, I'd settled in to examine the catalog. I read that in order to be accepted into one of the poetry workshops a student had to submit a portfolio of poems, five in all. I didn't have any poems, but I wanted an A, so I set myself the task of writing some. I had with me a book of essays by a woman named Alicia Suskin Ostriker. She was a feminist writer, a poet, and she'd written a book about women's poetry. I was reading it for a paper I was writing for another class, but sitting there, the soft Berkeley air floating temperately around me, I started learning what was happening in the world of contemporary poetry.

After thumbing through the book for an hour or so, I felt ready, so I wrote: three very strange poems. It was an exhausting effort and I resolved to write the other two later. When I finished with all five of the poems, I would submit them to the office, where I imagined kindly, gray-haired men would thumb through the several submissions before making up lists of the students they wanted to accept.

And I suppose that's when it started in earnest, the compulsion—as I waited for those lists. I'd run up to the third floor of Wheeler Hall, a giant, limestone edifice, as formal and placid as I imagined Greek buildings had been in Aristotle's day, push my face to the bulletin board, and stare, thinking the lists might miraculously appear if I groveled long and hard enough. I felt like the people who didn't survive in the movie *Alien*. The same pressure, or so I imagined, just under the skin. A little tense, a pulsing, shooting current in the throat. The compulsion was something like nerves, something like nausea, and the only way to assuage it was to run up those stairs, repeatedly, irrationally. To be accepted in a special class—it was a step up from a mere A, which by this time I was more than expert in acquiring. It was clubby, a clique. The writers' clique, and it never even crossed my mind that my attitude was awful.

When I first saw the Poet who accepted me into his class, I thought that he looked like an angel. He had a sweet face—pale blue eyes, curling lips, his nose just a little upturned. He was, I soon learned, very popular among the other students, and on the first day I sat in his class, I noticed he had groupies. They were preening and bespectacled. (I think they were trying to look like him, an attempt that failed in every case.) They'd drape themselves over their chairs, and look on at the Poet with a languid sort of revery, as if by taking him in with their eyes they might be bodily transformed. The Poet, for his part, seemed oblivious to this treatment. He'd sit there, gazing out at us, who sat in a circle of fifteen in the special room where all the workshops met. It was a stuffy place, the size of a kitchen (indeed, it had a fridge and sink) with tall, glowing windows that would let in pretty morning light.

I assessed the Poet's countenance very carefully that first day of class. He seemed a nice man. Like a father. He reminded me of my father, sitting in his den, avoiding everything besides his work, and I imagined him, the Poet, sitting in his study, in his house in the green hills of Berkeley, thumbing through his poetry, which would be marvelous, listening to Chopin. He was wearing a billowy oxford shirt, a pair of ratty khaki pants, and in this, too, he looked like my father, who wore similar ensembles. Both the Poet and my father lived so much in their heads, their incredibly overstuffed heads, and I imagined that behind the Poet's face there was an entire apparatus—cogs, little whistles, and levers for making ideas.

For the rest of the semester, we'd gather in a circle, the distressed '70s furniture sagging around us, the poster of Virginia Woolf, her neck white and twisted, peeling gently off the wall.

The Poet said hardly a thing, but his happy face beamed—plaintively, *lyrically*—as if to reassure us that we were, to a one, very brilliant, the smartest of the lot. No matter what it was we wrote, he'd smile and say something like: "This is terrifically odd!" or "What wonderful imagery!" The class was like a dream, and I repeated it the next semester, and the next semester after that. It was through this yearslong process, which resembled, as I see it now, an arranged marriage, that I fell in love with writing. Through no particular volition of my own, I began to understand the fact that the art was not the grade, that art in fact couldn't be graded.

There is a point when the rational becomes the irrational, when those things one does to survive in daily life become useless, even harmful. Grade grubbing is one of these things, and I understood this to a degree. The most interesting types of people aren't much drawn to grade grubbers, and the most fascinating intellects of any given period tend not to have been grade grubbers. The thing is, I didn't really think of myself as a grade grubber, seeing as I'd done so poorly in high school. In my mind I was trying to make something up because I felt like a failure.

As I was focusing so strenuously on getting my A's, my writing the place I would go to unwind, my siblings and my mother were living in Las Vegas, enjoying their highest times to date. The betting office (which I hadn't yet seen) was pumping out money, and my sister and brother were beating their tables in the room at the Mirage. They were going out to dinner, buying specialty Italian shirts, spending money on facials and personal trainers, but I hardly ever saw them. I was simply too focused on school.

The one person I did speak with and see on a regular basis was my father. He was paying my tuition, and I felt that I owed him for that. I treated my schoolwork like a job, him as my boss, and even though he didn't put any real pressure on me to get good grades, I would phone him up the moment I received my report card and blurt out every single one. I don't remember speaking with him about the rest of the family, but I don't remember much of those years but the grades.

· · ·

By the time I had entered my junior year, my father had remarried. His wife was a congenial younger woman who had many things in common with him. They liked the same shows, the same music and books, and whenever I'd visit, the two of them would take me out to dinner or a movie, talk about the snow, about how envious they were that the rest of the family had left for the temperate West.

It was around this time that my preoccupation with grades became a serious problem. I'd been taking a full load of classes each semester, and had attended summer school three summers in a row. I had a year's worth of extra credits, but I didn't want to graduate. I wanted to stay in school forever. I thought that I'd probably go to grad school, but I couldn't decide between English and anthropology. I was also considering getting an MFA in poetry, a degree I liked the idea of but that I knew would be financially impractical. In order to keep my options open, I undertook the writing of two separate theses. I also signed up for the Graduate Record Exams.

Because I'd taken on such an unrealistic load of work, I forfeited any sort of social life I may have had, spending all my days in the belly of the main campus library, which, like all the other buildings on campus, was as giant and gray as some prehistoric dinosaur, all my nights curling up with *The Princeton Review's Book of Graduate Record Exams.* My favorite section was the logic:

> Eight guards—Stoddard, Thorpe, Udell, Vaughn, Westbrook, Xavier, Yates, and Zacharias—are guarding a valuable gem. They are stationed around the gem, equally spaced, in a circular formation. The following is known about their positions:
>
> Westbrook and Xavier must be stationed next to each other.
>
> Zacharias and Udell must be stationed next to each other.
>
> Stoddard must be stationed directly across the circle from Yates.

And then there would be questions:

> All of the following guards could be stationed immediately next to Udell EXCEPT
>
> (a) Stoddard
>
> (b) Thorpe
>
> (c) Vaughn
>
> (d) Xavier
>
> (e) Yates

> If Stoddard is stationed next to Zacharias, and if Xavier is stationed next to Yates, which one of the following people must be stationed directly across from Xavier?

```
(a) Stoddard
(b) Udell
(c) Westbrook
(d) Yates
(e) Zacharias
```

How I loved the orderliness of these questions and the certainty of their answers. I would practice with alacrity. I loved those little tests!

My theses were something else altogether, so much harder. They were simply not as easy to master as either the GREs or typical academic classes. For the first, in English, I was writing on the famously difficult modernist poet Gertrude Stein, and I'd sit in my bedroom and read her repetitive verses for hours, my brain like an old, broken record.

The second thesis, in anthropology, was not only intellectually difficult, but emotionally trying as well. Throughout my years at Berkeley, I'd been a student of aesthetics and also of medical anthropology, and in order to draw on both fields, I had chosen for my thesis the topic of medical photography. My idea was to address the history of the field, its original assumptions, and how they had changed by comparing photographs of gynecological patients from the first half of the twentieth century with photographs of AIDS patients from the second half. In order to research my topic, I would go to the library of the School of Public Health, a foreboding brick building, and peruse the shelves of medical textbooks. I would pick a book at random, thumb through its waxy and mildew-flecked pages, and gaze on at diseased and deformed genitalia, which would pop out at the eyes like rotten fruit.

Unlike the English project, which I had only the spring to

complete, the anthropology project lasted for the entire year, and as the months wore on, I began to develop various medical symptoms of my own, the most worrisome of which, in my view, was that my hair was falling out. Strand after strand would shipwreck itself on my fingers, and my comb was like a thickly woven rug. I went to the doctor and told her I was balding.

"That's highly unusual," she replied, placing her hands on my head. I repeated my symptoms, certain that she wasn't understanding their severity.

"Sometimes it's stress," she said. "That can make your hair fall out. A temporary thing." She asked me how things had been going, and I told her about my work, that I sat in the library of the School of Public Health all day long, looking at medical textbooks.

"Well, you know," she said, "there is a psychological condition, very well documented. When a person spends a lot of time around sick people or even just learning about them, they'll develop phantom symptoms of their own. The power of suggestion, you know." She then handed me a regular white envelope and told me to collect all my hairs for a week. One hundred per day was the average.

During the week that followed, I kept fanatical track of my hairs, pulling them out of my head during class, picking them off of my shirts before bed. I wanted to be absolutely certain, and seeing as Berkeley was known as a radical, forgiving sort of place, I didn't think the woman in front of me in the line at the café would mind if I bent down, picked a hair off the floor, and put it in my crumpled white security envelope. At the end of each day, I would count out my hairs, then put them carefully into a separate envelope on which I'd mark the day's number in ink. When I went back to the doctor, I happily informed her she'd been right all along, that I hadn't been balding. I was just a hypochondriac.

That spring I took a trip to Las Vegas, in part to get away from my too stressful studies. The part of the trip that I am able to remember best is waiting in line at McCarran to return to U.C. Berkeley. Howard was with me, standing to my right. Both of us were gazing at the airplanes taking off, their silver-gray abdomens smoking. I was thinking to myself that I never could have been good at aeronautics, not with my horrible math scores.

"I got my GRE scores back," I said. "I did so incredibly badly in math."

"How did you do on everything else?" Howard asked.

"Logic was my best score. You know, I thought I'd do better in English."

"Why?"

"Because it's my *major*. I mean, what does logic do? What's that good for?"

"Well, you might be good at poker, for one," Howard replied.

I stared at him and laughed at him. His expression didn't budge.

"You're not kidding," I remarked.

"No, I'm not kidding. It's all logic—logic and psychology. You don't need math."

I hadn't thought much about playing, but I hadn't not thought about it either.

"You don't need math?"

"No, you can just memorize the basic odds, and any math you'd have to do at the table is simple enough. There are only fifty-two cards in the deck and the odds tend to repeat themselves—the same sorts of numbers, the same types of problems. One out of five to hit a flush with a card still to come on the end; one out of two that a pair will appear on the board by the fifth card, and so on and so forth."

"I don't understand anything you're saying," I said. "But I believe you."

"The thing you really need the most is a logical mind." Howard was excited now, spurred on by our poker talk. "Yeah, I've seen those questions like they have on that test. Those are good questions. If you can answer those questions correctly, you can probably answer other questions correctly, like what someone's holding when they've bet on the end, there's an ace on the board, and the last card to hit was a two. Yeah, the more I think about it, the more poker's just like those questions on that test, and if you made a lot of money, you could write in the day and play poker at night."

"You really think so?" I said, imagining myself sitting by some sparkling pool, the sun blazing down on my face as I scratched lines of beautiful poetry onto a page.

"Sure," Howard said. "You should come out and try."

11 ♠ One of Them

My mother wasn't happy when I told her I was coming.

"I thought you'd be the *normal* one," she said. "I don't *want* another gambler."

"But I don't really want to gamble, that's not why I'm coming, I just want to write."

"What's the difference?" she said. "It's all weirdness, just *weirdness,* and I don't know what happened. I thought you were going to go on in school. . . ."

"Do you not want me to come? Do you not want me there?"

"No, no, I want you here. But can't you at least get a job in a casino? As a waitress or something?"

"I want to make money. I want to make money and write."

"But you won't have a life, don't you see? And that matters. It's impossible here—all the tourists and the players, who are rotten to a one. You know, just the other day I was working in the office, it was really late at night, and one of the callers came in and asked me for money—for money, from me, the accountant!—'Can I have a twenty?' he said, and I handed it to him, I just did, even though I knew that he'd go out and spend it on coke."

"Well, who cares . . ."

"And then when you go out to look for a regular job—which you will, eventually, I guarantee it, because you'll get bored—you'll have nothing to put on your résumé. Just your old A's, that'll be it, and they'll ask you in the interview, 'So what have you been doing in the last couple of years,' and you'll have to tell them you played poker, that that was all you'd done, and they'll laugh at you and say to you, 'Well, thank you but no thank you.' And then you'll have to take some entry-level, awful job, some job that you're too old to have. . . ."

"But that's not the point. I just want to make money."

"But this is different. It's *gambling*. And even if you know you'll eventually win, those ups and downs, those swings will affect you. I sometimes see Howard and Annie, they look so ravaged, do you want to look ravaged at the end of the day?"

"I don't know," I replied. "No."

"And then you'll go home and you'll sleep and in the morning, when you sit down at the keyboard in order to write, you know what you'll be thinking about?"

"What?"

"That final hand, that very final hand, the one where you lost all your money. And you'll write about money, or you won't write at all, because you'll call up your brother and ask him to tell you what it was you did wrong. And you'll spend all your time going over your hands, like the other players do, because that's how you get good."

"I don't want to discuss it. I've made my decision. I'm coming," I said.

"Oh, all right," said my mother. "I'm just trying to tell you it's hard."

Though I knew that my mother had the practical opinion, that my plan to play poker was unusual to say the least, it seemed to me the most obvious route I could take upon finishing school. In my junior year at Berkeley, I'd attended an English department commencement (the classes were so large that they'd have to hold separate graduations for each of the majors), and the address that I'd heard there had convinced me I needed to exercise my options—all of them—before relinquishing my dream of writing poetry. It had been held at the Greek, a 10,000 seat amphitheater where, on the weekends, some rock bands would play. Phish, Tracy Chapman. I'd been there just once, to see Alanis Morissette, but now here I was, in the bright afternoon, gazing up at a writer named Maxine Hong Kingston, who'd taught in the department for years. A small Asian woman with a head of long and straight white hair, she was standing at the lectern, her hands up in the air, instructing the members of the class to be true to their ideals. I remember looking out across the plane of flat black hats, knowing I had just one year, just a year to figure out what it was that I should do, and my brother's remarks at McCarran had assuaged so many fears at once—that I'd never have money, that I'd have to work a nine-to-five, that I'd never be close to my family again—it seemed to me the ideal thing.

There was also the fact I'd been offered a mansion to live in for free. The salmon-colored, stucco-covered bunker of a box belonged to Z, who'd purchased the property in order to have a place to stay when he traveled to Las Vegas. Even after paying a name-dropping interior designer a hefty sum to decorate, however, he hardly ever slept there, preferring instead to take rooms at the Mirage, which were closer to the action. This was a decadent development for me, of course, and as I drove through the property gates, parked my rusted-out Honda in the half-moon driveway, and gazed up at the grand oak double doors, I felt a little woozy. The shrubs to either side of me seemed to be giggling, goading me into the box. The pool, which was uselessly small but for dipping one's toe, seemed to lap and lap against the walls, creaking in the cool night air, and then there was the sound of the catalpa leaves, rustling and shedding, rustling and shedding.

Once I gained entrance to the box and was inside, I was stunned by how clean and untouched the place was. In front of me was a vast expanse of cream marble flooring punctuated by two paisley-patterned love seats and a shiny black table, upon which a stealthy-looking stereo blipped. To my left was an airy French-style kitchen, with cabinets made of clean blond wood, and little flowered counter tiles. I stacked my beat-up Crate & Barrel dishes in a cabinet near the stove, and then set about walking the maze of dark rooms, looking for a place to sleep. Through one of the corridors, there was a study lined on all sides with empty bookshelves, and beyond that, a parlor over which a broken wide-screen TV loomed. Next to the parlor, there was a senselessly narrow room furnished with twin beds and bureau. It looked like the rooms that I'd known at St. Paul's, its gentility vaguely offensive to me, and so I moved on, to the second wing of the house, where I finally found a place to rest. The master bedroom, which had been originally designed for Z's girlfriend, Grace, was tasteful and immaculate. The headboard was formal and floral-patterned and the carpet was as white as dried bone. For those first months I spent learning poker in Vegas, I would carefully sleep on the top of the bedspread for fear I would sully the beautiful sheets.

• • •

It wasn't until the next morning that Howard finally phoned. He'd left a small pile of poker how-to books on the counter and he wanted to know if I'd found them.

"Yes," I replied. "Can we discuss them over dinner? I'm really eager to get started."

"Sure," Howard said. "Let's meet up at the buffet—around seven?"

I had always been a canny mimic, and I thought that watching Howard play in my tiny, two-bit game might help me improve. "When we're done, will you give me a lesson?"

"I don't think so," he said. "We all play alone. You wouldn't understand the moves I'd make in any case, since you don't have a lot of experience." I persisted, however, and after some haggling, we struck a deal: he would play at the $20–$40 stakes table for exactly one hour while I watched and asked questions. After that he would have to go practice his golf for a bet that he'd made with a friend.

The only other time I'd played poker had been back in California, at a fluorescent-lit card room called the Oaks Club. It was just a few miles from Berkeley and was a hangout for frat boys and locals. When I first walked into the club, it was assumed I was there to meet a boyfriend or husband, and no one had been willing to help me. Finally, after I had wandered around the room for some time, a raisin-skinned waitress had pointed me back toward the cage to buy chips (called a "cage" since the window is typically barred).

Once I'd purchased my rack of fifty one-dollar chips, I'd walked to the pit and settled down at the lowest-staked table in the room: 50¢ for the first two rounds of betting, $1 per round on the end. To my left slouched a man with a do rag on his head and thick rings on each of his long, bony fingers. To my right napped a very old lady, who'd missed the big blind (the ante in a Hold 'Em game) for more than an hour, but whom no one was willing to expel (there wasn't much of a list). Directly across from me, ensconced in a big cloud of smoke, sat a little Chinese woman who, because she sucked down several packs a day, was referred to as the Dragon Lady. She would show up every afternoon and play at the lowest-staked table. A player would be lucky to take home $100 in a night at such a table, but the Dragon Lady played for keeps. Not that she would really play. She would mostly just wait, her hand moving mechanically from the ashtray to her mouth, her eyes staring coolly at the baize. She was careful, to a fault, and whenever she threw down a $1 chip, you knew what she was holding. Aces, kings, or queens.

"You come out from college?" she rasped.

"Yes."

"What you do here?"

"I want to learn poker."

"You'll never beat the Dragon Lady," one of the other players said. "She plays tight."

"I no play tight," the Dragon Lady said. "You just mad that I beat you last hand."

"Aw, I could never be mad at you, Dragon Lady," the man said.

I played her just one hand that day, the first I ever played. She'd called the 50¢ ante, not raising her aces. I held the jack-ten of hearts, and so called. Three other people had entered the pot, but no one had raised. When the first three cards (called "the flop") appeared Qh-2h-7s, the player in the one-seat checked, the Dragon Lady bet, and two people behind her had folded. I'd called, since I had a good draw.

When the fourth card had come a four of hearts, making my flush, I couldn't seem to trust my eyes.

"You stay in hand," the Dragon Lady said. "I no like that. You need get out of this hand." What did she have? Was I crazy? Was she? When the final card hit—a blank—she checked, leaving the betting up to me—I chickened out.

"I also check," I said, pressing my hand to the table.

When we turned our cards over, the Dragon Lady laughed at me. "You saved me some money," she said. "You had the best hand! You need bet on the end!"

I could tell from the promotional copy on their covers that the books Howard had left me were the classics. There was one very slim and very glossy book called *Hold-'Em Poker for Beginners*, by David Sklansky, which cataloged the basic rules of how to play, and how to win. On the cover, there were pictures of gray cartoonish guns, which promised the reader a Wild West experience, though, by this point, the mid-1990s, poker had become a more mainstream pursuit. No longer the province of cowboys and mobsters, it had become not only acceptable but fashionable among the upper classes, and I supposed that Sklansky's cover was actually a signal to the people, like me, who were angling to *feel* Wild West. Regardless of its cover, however, I read through the book with the utmost attention. It was, I knew, the true Bible of poker, the place where I'd find all the basic statistics—the rules, the procedures, the various odds. I committed to memory all that I could, copying out all the hands I could start with, then putting the book in a drawer for my later perusal.

The second book in the pile was a gargantuan hardcover called *Super/System: A Course in Power Poker,* written by "Texas Dolly" Doyle Brunson, the Jabba-the-Hut-like creature who dominated my brother's table. The cover was midnight blue with a golden etching of the then golden boy running to shoot a slam-dunk. As a young man, Doyle had been a star basketball player, but since those lanky early years, his body had accommodated so many slices of chocolate cake (he had a habit of gorging on sweets when he lost) that it had grown to look like a lumpy and overstuffed pillow. The only parts of his body that remained nimble were his hands, and whenever Doyle would pull his pots in, these would flare out like the sheathing on a cobra's head, enveloping the pile of slippery chips.

It was easy to see, from just a quick glance through its 600-plus pages, that *Super/System* was not a book for beginners. In it Doyle outlined everything he'd learned in his several decades of playing poker professionally. In a further bid for thoroughness, he'd enlisted help from his friends, each of whom was a legend in the world of poker. There was "Crazy Mike" Caro, who'd made a reputation for himself as a master of poker statistics; Bobby "The Owl" Baldwin, who would later be the one to convince the Mirage's management to establish their lavish, high-stakes poker room; Amarillo "Slim" Preston, who had the elongated charm of a poker-playing Gumby; David "Chip"

Reese, who would later be the youngest player inducted into the Poker Hall of Fame; and David "Einstein" Sklansky, who'd written the excellent book for beginners I'd ingested just that morning. Howard had told me that most beginners lose a lot of money at the start because they get too creative with their cards, trying to bluff and feint and slow-play winning hands, so I decided to save *Super/System* for later, when I had a better handle on the basics of the game.

The last book in the pile was, like the first, written by one of Doyle's guest experts, "Crazy Mike" Caro. It was titled *Caro's Book of Tells*. Inside were a number of grainy, black-and-white photos of people playing cards, each of which illustrated some common tell (a gesture or expression that gives a player's hand away) or other. I read through the prefaces and forewords first, taking in the basic concepts of poker—concepts that, though I had a dim awareness of them before reading the book, I'd never before seen so clearly articulated in print. In a section called "Nonverbal Lying," on page 13 of the book's "Original Foreword" (which had been written by one David M. Hayano, Ph.D.), I read:

> We must first see that everything poker players do while sitting at the table—betting, checking, calling, raising, bluffing—involves movement or behavior of one kind or another. Furthermore, we can assume that poker behavior is indicative of mood or emotion, and that players may reveal their hidden, internal psychological states by how they act. For example, bluffing can be considered to be a kind of nonverbal lying, one that many poker players do not always carry off successfully. Like a verbal lie, they are found out and must pay the penalties. We are then

> ready to allow for the fact that in the study of poker behavior, various "mistakes" or "clues" may be found.

And later:

> The practical advantages of spotting tells is obvious; Your poker skills and monetary gains will increase dramatically. With *Mike Caro's Book of Tells* in hand, a truly original book in its field, we can finally get a glimpse of the ways by which we can sort out the hard-to-read liars and bluffers across the table from our other more predictable foes. We are on our first step in poker toward being able to determine the truth.

The chapters themselves were structured something like Dale Carnegie's hugely popular book *How to Win Friends and Influence People,* each including small boxed "rules" or "laws" that summed up the chapter's main findings. In a chapter entitled "Glancing at Chips," I read: "A player glances secretly at his chips only when he's considering a bet—and almost always because he helped his hand (Caro's Law of Tells #8)," and in another (entitled "Nervousness"): "In the absence of indications to the contrary, call any bettor whose hand covers his mouth (Caro's Law of Tells #5)." When taken on their own, each of these "laws" seemed rather useless and vague, but as a group they made a kind of perfect sense. Whether lying or telling the truth, people were always betraying their desires. I spent the rest of the afternoon poring over "Crazy Mike" Caro's strange book, impatient to see all his theorems in action, and at half past the hour, the moon like a tiny white flashlight behind me, I got in my car and drove west.

12 ♠ Tells

When I first walked into the buffet to meet Howard, I felt as if I were entering the company cafeteria. The walls were covered in a pink floral paper that matched both the chairs and the plastic bougainvillea. A short-skirted hostess directed me to a table near the food line and as I waited for Howard, I stared at a middle-aged woman dining to my right. She had a very large chin and was hovering over a big plate of food. I remember the way she balked when my brother walked in, her door of a jaw falling open. It was easy for me to forget—had always been easy—that other people were menaced by Howard. He was six foot five, more than three hundred pounds, and I doubted anyone would have imagined that he was deeply engrossed in the animal-liberation classic *Diet for a New America,* and that, with all his height and girth, he hadn't ingested an animal product in years.

Because both my brother and I adhered to such a strict form of vegetarianism, the buffet wasn't quite the smorgasbord it might have been. The fluorescent Key lime pie, the dripping, fresh-hewn steak, even the boatloads of wilted pink shrimp were off-limits to us, and so we satisfied ourselves with Spanish rice and bits of lettuce. It was over such a meal that Howard started quizzing me on the basics of poker—how to figure odds, how to bluff, the criteria for folding. In response to his questions, I ticked off statistics and starting requirements without hesitation.

"But do you understand all the things that you're saying?" he asked. "Do you really understand why it's not a good idea to play a queen-jack combination before the flop? Or why a guy who has his hands turned toward his chips is probably holding some pretty good cards?"

"Yes. You don't want to play the queen-jack because, even though they're pretty little face cards, it's too easy to lose the hand to a queen or a jack with a higher second card, even if you make your pair."

"Right."

"And when the guy has his hands turned in toward his chips, it means he *wants* to put them in the pot. He's not even worried about it, and that means he's not bluffing."

"And what if his hands are turned outward?"

"Then he's bluffing."

"Or he's read *The Book of Tells* and has guessed that you have too."

"Double-bluffing."

"I mean, you never *really* know anything." My brother put a piece of sautéed onion in his mouth. "It's all just situation."

"Just the feeling."

"That's right. And the thing you have to do, the thing you have to do that can be hard is to keep your brain in the game and not to analyze too much, because you've just gotta go with the flow, get a feel for the room, get a feel for the table you're playing." He paused. "Because sometimes things just won't feel right and you won't know quite why and your brain will be saying you're a favorite to win, when really, in the end, your hand's already dead."

The poker room itself, like everything else in the Mirage, was modeled after a South Seas thatch hut. That was the casino's theme—Brazil, South America, the tropics—and every time I entered the place, the atmosphere would soothe my nerves, drenching my face and my body in its scrupled air. After walking the bright, breezy hallway, down through the blackjack and baccarat pits, I'd arrive at the poker room, ready to purchase my $200 rack and play cards.

The feature I liked best about the card room was its utter orderliness. The tables, roughly thirty, were organized according to their stakes. The smallest-staked tables, like the $3–$6 Hold 'Em game, at which I played, were generally flush up against the rail separating the room from the rest of the casino, where any passersby could take glances at the action before going on their way to the buffet or to their tables. Middle-limit games, like $20–$40 Omaha and $15–$30 Stud, were played in the center of the room, closer to the cage and to the bathrooms, while the really high-stakes games, like the $300–$600 Hold 'Em that my brother and sister specialized in, could be found only at the very back of the room on an elevated platform away from both the rails and other players.

Unlike many of the other players in my game, I was perfectly happy to sit at my lowly rail-buffeting table. I simply didn't deserve to be any higher until I improved my play, and I never did understand those players who would complain about their standing in the room. Either you won and moved up in the stakes, or you lost and stayed put. Those were the rules, and I had a real faith in the system. I'd been witness to Howard's ascent from the 50¢–$1 game at the Bar Point to the $300–$600 game at the Mirage. It had taken him nearly twelve years to move up through those limits.

Annie's ascent had been so much quicker that by the time I arrived in Las Vegas, the pace of her progress was the talk of the room. I remember once sitting down at my table and assessing the faces of my peers. One of them, Carl, had been staring straight back. He was an ugly man, maybe fifty years old, and had never said a word as far as I can recall. His skin appeared smooth, like a placid curtain, his eyes wide and bright. He smiled at me then, the skin on his face drawing open as if to let in morning light, and said: "Your sister took a helluva lot of money from me when she was playing down here in the pit, and I'm glad that you've chosen to come here and give that money back." The corners of his mouth had fallen then and his eyes had gone dull and it had seemed he was really a robot, not a person at all.

Just as Howard was about to quiz me further on various odds, his phone started ringing. He'd placed a million on the games that night—an unusually large, though not extraordinary, figure—and he was down $300,000.

"Why do you have to bet sports?" I asked.

"Are you kidding?"

"It just seems so risky and it makes you upset."

"Do you know how much money we can make in a season?"

"No."

"Well, it's a lot."

"But why do you need it, when you already win playing poker?"

"It's all in the edges, Katy, and the more money I can put into play, the more I can win, and the more I can win, the more I can bet, and so even if the edges remain constant in terms of their percentage of advantage—two and a half percent if I'm really lucky—I'll make more and more money. Does that make sense?" Howard polished off his plate and then dialed up the hotline for the fifth time that night, and then, just minutes later, for the sixth.

The only other time I remembered seeing Howard in such a funk was at a Super Bowl party that David, a recent addition to the betting group, had thrown. The house, located near a desolate highway on the outskirts of the city, was empty except for a couple of wide-screened TVs and some ugly brown couches. I'd flown in from Berkeley to visit my brother, and, seeing as he'd bet $100,000 on the outcome of the game, I'd had little choice but to accompany him to the party. All the elite of the Las Vegas gambling world were there, and I remember sitting gingerly down on the couch, not daring to move. The room was so awash in that subtle combination of nerves and hope and awful dread that comes of large wagers that I felt like I had to swim through a kind of mental lard just to go to the bathroom. When the game finally started, the entire room exploded into cheers. Half the room had bet on Dallas, half on the Bills, and as the game progressed, the party bifurcated according to teams, one side in the living room, the other in the den. By half-time, my brother was down $50,000, but as the game came to a conclusion, he was up a few thousand—enough that he took me out to a sumptuous sushi dinner, where he relished his order of vegan kapa maki.

In the end, it wasn't altogether impossible for me to adjust to the gambler's relationship with his action, for it resembles to a close degree the writer's relationship with his writing. When things are going well, all is cheerful and bright in the world, but when things are going badly, a glumness comes to dominate the atmosphere, like a tenebrous cloud hanging over your head, intermittently storming. No matter the fluctuations in outcome or mood, however, the absolute worst thing imaginable is to never again be in action, to never again write a word; that would be like death, which, no matter what your stake or expectation, is infinitely worse than waiting for your luck to turn.

By the time our dinner at the Mirage ended, Howard's fortunes had reversed. With all but one of the games over, he found himself a big winner for the night: "What are we waiting for?" he said. (As if I had been the one waiting on the outcome of something as out of my control as a basketball game!) "Let's go give you your lesson."

· · ·

It was the day before New Year's, and with Mike Tyson in town for a fight, the poker room was packed. As Howard led me to the cage, where he kept a box full of ivory and lavender $5,000 chips, I felt as if I were in a New York City subway, the heat of many bodies suffusing the quivering air. After signing his box out and pocketing $10,000 (just two of his pretty matte chips), he walked me to his table, which, because it was the highest-staked in the room, was far back in the corner, where spectators (known as "railbirds" after their habit of standing by the railings and gawking) weren't allowed to go. Realizing there wasn't a single opening at any one of the tables, Howard led me over to the High Brush, a tall Italianate man in a double-breasted suit who organized the games and cleaned the tables (thus the designation "brush") when a game was dispersed.

Howard asked if he could play over someone else, which meant that that person had gone to dinner or a show and had left the seat temporarily open.

"Sure," said the man, walking over to the cage, where he picked up a clear plastic box. "What kind of game are you looking for?"

"Twenty to forty dollars, maybe forty to eighty. I'm just trying to show my sister a few plays."

"Another sister, heh?" the Brush said. "What are you trying to do, take the place over?"

"Something like that," Howard said.

Every poker game has its unique nimbus, and as the two of us settled in, I could see that, aside from one regular pro, and one equally regular compulsive, the majority of the players were tourists. There was a quick chemistry to such a combination: the pro would take from the tourists, and the tourists would take from the compulsive. It was like a Ponzi scheme, or like musical chairs. Even the compulsive would sometimes take a pot.

"Pull your chair closer," Howard said. "I'm going to flip up my cards at the corners so you can see what I'm holding, but don't make any faces when I do so, OK?"

"OK," I said, inching forward.

"Now," said Howard, maneuvering his fingers around the plastic box (which was used to protect the absentee player's stack of chips). "What I want you to do is forget about Sklansky's odds for now and just pay attention to body language."

"OK," I replied.

"I don't want you to pay attention to my cards at all. They don't matter. What matters is what you see—what *everyone* can see."

"Right," I said, nodding my head.

"And if you start to think too hard about your cards, then you can't focus on what's really going on, which has *nothing* to do with your cards but which has *everything* to do with your opponent's cards and what's going on in his head." Howard sat up straight and looked around. "Do you understand what I'm saying?" I remember staring not at his eyes, but rather at his hair, which was bristling with patches of new gray.

"Yes, I understand," I said.

The first hand was dealt, and Howard flipped up his cards at the corners so I could see them. They were junk: an eight of hearts and a queen of spades.

"I'm the last to have to act," Howard said. "So let's see what these monkeys want to do." As the action came around to Howard, everyone folded, everyone but a tourist from Arkansas, who called. Howard raised. "Not a lot of competition," he remarked. "And even if he calls my raise, I've taken the lead on the hand, which, in almost every case, is going to be the right thing to do."

Seeing my brother put his chips in the pot, the tourist from Arkansas slumped. His sunglasses slid down the bridge of his nose, and his forehead broke out in a thick, shiny layer of sweat. He wanted to play, but he hated his cards, and this split in motivation tore visibly at his resolve. "I'll call you," he said.

The flop was dealt: a king of spades, an ace of clubs, and a two of diamonds. Junk for my brother, and junk for the tourist, who checked. Howard bet.

The tourist shook his head. "You got me beat, eh?" he said, but he called the bet in any case. He wanted very badly to play. He had come all the way to Las Vegas to do so, and Howard, who had nothing, was happy to oblige him.

When the next card came, a three of spades, Howard immediately bet. The tourist stared intensely at the pot. Whatever he had, it was almost certainly better than my brother's lone queen, but he had no way to know this, and he threw down his cards.

"Did you see how that worked?" Howard asked, leaning back and stacking up his chips.

"Yes," I replied. "Your opponent didn't like his cards, so it didn't really matter what you had. You could have had nothing and he still would have folded."

"That's right," Howard said.

The next hand Howard played was, like the first, based on nothing. He turned his cards up at the corner: a king-five suited. His new opponent was sitting to his left, lips red and pouty, wrapped morosely around a Capri. At the start of the hour, her husband had stopped by. When she'd seen him, she'd brightened, but he'd come just to tell her he was sitting at the bar on the other side of the rain forest. Did she need any money? "No," she whispered, shaking her bottle-blond head. *"No, I don't need any money."*

She opened the hand, and since the next six people folded to her left, Howard raised.

"I want to get her all to myself," he said.

She called his raise. The flop was dealt:

6♠ 9♥ 3♠

The woman looked sullenly at my brother. "Check," she said.

"Bet," said my brother, trying to take the pot forcibly.

"Call," she said, spilling some $5 chips on the table.

The next card came. A ten of hearts. A glimmer appeared in the woman's eye. She'd caught something. "Bet," she said.

"Raise," Howard said.

The woman blinked and blinked her eyes.

"Call," she said, putting a $100 chip in the pot. *"Call,"* she repeated.

The next card came.

"Queen of diamonds."

The woman bet.

"Raise," Howard said.

The woman then crumpled. She pressed her lips around her cigarette and took a feeble drag. She sat like that, for a very long time, and I could imagine her, sitting in just the same position, at her kitchen table at home or in the front seat of a car or in a lawn chair on the beach at Martha's Vineyard, her husband never there.

"Tens are *never* good," she said, relinquishing her hand.

An hour had passed and our lesson was over. It was nearly ten o'clock at night, but still it felt early.

"I have to practice for my golf bet," Howard mumbled, standing up. "You can come if you want."

The bet was that Howard and a friend of his would get a better score than their poker rival, John. Whoever won the bet would be paid a lot of money.

"I need to practice every day." Howard handed off a tip to

the valet. We then drove to the Las Vegas Golf Club, which was out near the airport, parked the car, paid the fee, and went in.

"Just one bucket of balls and we'll go."

I sat down on a long green bench and watched as Howard fed the giant golf ball machine some crisp dollars. I could hear the dollars go in smoothly, then the plunking of balls as they filled up the bucket. Howard picked up the bucket, spread the balls across the well-trimmed grass, then proceeded to drive them as far as he could toward the bright yellow flag.

"Think they make good money on these?" he asked, pointing greedily at the balls. "Ten cents apiece and they use them again and again."

Zooming back and forth across the field was a junket, which would pick up the balls through its long sucking roller. Even with the constant zooming back and forth, the retriever had missed a few spots, and these were covered in what, from a distance, appeared to be flushes of white confetti. I could hear a subtle flapping sound, of the tattered yellow flags being whipped by the wind, and the planes, which would hover above the vast range before flying out over the Luxor.

Driving next to Howard was a tall Asian man, wearing golf shoes and navy sweats. He was driving his balls as far out as he could, no real aim, no direction. I thought to myself that the man must come down to the golf range like this late at night to relax.

"Let me try," I said, as I got off the bench and pulled a club out of the bag.

"OK, just do it over here, where I can keep an eye on your form," Howard said. I had never hit a golf ball before.

I missed. The air flew from my lungs.

"Let me show you," said Howard as he came up behind me and adjusted my fingers on the handle of the club.

"Here, you take it," I said. "You're the one with the bet."

"But it's good if I show you. . . ."

"But your time is worth money. And I'm tired and I want to go home."

Howard laughed. "Just this bucket," he said. "Just these last few ridiculously overpriced balls."

13 ♠ *PokerWorld*

In the months just before I arrived in Las Vegas, my sister and brother and their poker-playing friends had come up with yet another scheme, another "edge," as my brother would have called it: they were going to publish a glossy startup magazine called *PokerWorld* and make a lot of money. The only other similar magazine, *Card Player*, was so pulpy and cheaply produced that they figured they could easily make off with their profits. And so, in spite of the fact that not one of them had worked an editorial day in their lives, they rented an office on the south side of town, hired some people to publish and design their new venture, and enlisted my sister (with her English degree) to be editor-in-chief. Since I too had a background in English, I was offered the position of editorial assistant, and though I knew it was risky to work under Annie, I accepted the job. Not only would it allow me to bankroll my poker, it would also assuage all the doubts my mother had about my résumé.

Though my duties at the magazine included proofreading, writing, and editing, what I really did was baby-sit. Annie had recently given birth to a little girl named Maud, who had a tuft of fine brown hair and an antic disposition, and she insisted on taking her to work so she could breast-feed. No matter that Annie had a mountain of toys in one corner of her office, the baby would get bored, and it was left up to me to entertain her.

I remember one day. Maud had crawled up to the window in the back, put her hand to the glass, and started to scream. Maybe she'd strained her eyes looking up at the sun, or maybe she'd seen something frightening. Whatever it was, she had burst into tears and I'd spent the past half hour making efforts to distract her.

"Dugggie," she gurgled as I held her in my arms and walked around in little circles. *"Dugggie, dugggie!"* She was pointing at the ugly pastel lithograph of a dog that dominated the small hallway between my sister's office and the bright back room. *"Dugggie!!"* I was holding her tightly, trying not to let her fall. It was hard for me, a twenty-two-year-old woman, to control little Maudie, who was one. *"Dugggie, dugggie, dugggie,"* she yelled. She then caught a glimpse of her reflection in the glass and started howling. "Mud. Mud." Her eyes were wide and baffled: "Mud!"

"No, it's 'Maud.' *Maaawwwd,*" I said, turning away from the glass.

"M*u*d. M*u*d!" She was pointing frantically, pulling away from my chest.

"How am I supposed to keep her from falling?" I yelled, wanting Annie to take her off my hands. "Would your investors be happy if they knew that your writer had been baby-sitting all morning?"

"Be quiet," Annie said. "I'm on the phone."

"This isn't my job," I replied. "My job is to proofread and write. Give me something to do!"

"Wait a second," she said, covering the mouthpiece with her hand. "*Please* give me a break. I'll talk to you when I'm through." I went back outside, to the hallway, sat down in a chair, and bounced the baby up and down.

"Now come in here and give her to me," Annie said, taking little Maudie in her arms. She then lifted the front of her shirt and exposed a crumpled aureole, which she put in Maudie's mouth. "I found some work for you to do. I want you to go to a fetish shop in town and buy a pair of handcuffs. We need them for a photo shoot tomorrow. We're putting them on the cover." I nodded. "And after that, if you feel like it, you can come by for dinner. Now will that make it up?"

For the first months I spent learning poker in Vegas, I would drive the Strip repeatedly, compulsively—on my way to work, then back again, after playing; in the morning when I went to get my coffee (though it wasn't anywhere near Z's); during lunch. I adored all the lights, especially in daytime, when the whole place appeared like some horrible hangover. I was, therefore, perfectly happy to drive down the Strip toward that part of Las Vegas where I knew I'd find handcuffs.

As I drove from the corner of Sunset and Viking, where the offices were, down to Flamingo, which breezed past a giant Hamada restaurant before passing a scary electrical grid, I would think about poker, about all of those things that I could have done better, the mistakes that I'd made. I'd been working for only a month in the office, but I already wanted to quit. I couldn't stand to baby-sit, and poker was my only other means of making money. I needed to get better.

When I got to the Strip and the MGM Grand, I turned right, went by Caesar's, the Mirage, Treasure Island, then a series of bright, blinking eyesores: the Frontier (which resembled a '70s high-rise), Circus Circus (with its hideous oversized clowns), and finally Westward Ho (the ugliest of all, with its fountains of dim yellow light). In spite of any hideousness, however, I was still quite in love with Las Vegas. I was madly in love with the money, and when I finally arrived at what amounted to a small municipality of adult stores, I rather giddily locked up my car.

Of the several emporia on that particular block, the one that looked most promising was called the Lusty Lady. When I walked in, I was shocked by their wares. There were tiny, flosslike leather thongs and wickedly sleek cat o' nine tails. Dildos, their plastic veins a dark pink, lined the walls like little soldiers. There were two people in that store, a man and a woman, who apparently owned it. They laughed at me and asked me what it was that I was looking for. I told them I was looking for handcuffs. "Not for me . . . and not for sex!" I said, blushing. "It's for the cover of a magazine." They nodded their heads and then pulled out a pink plastic package.

"These are all we got," said the man. He had a graying Vandyke and wrinkled forehead. I took the package in my hands and turned it around. The handcuffs looked small.

"They're for women," he said. "Not the real deal, like they'd use at the police station, you know." The key was shaped oddly, like a rather naughty heart, but I figured they would do all right.

• • •

Annie was standing in the middle of her kitchen with Maudie on one hip and her hand on the other. She was watching over a giant vat of lentils. It was her specialty. Lentils and spinach. The house smelled just awful, all that iron and pepper. I went out onto the patio.

In the back of Annie's house, which was the washed-out green of unripe limes, was a medium-sized lap pool. I decided I should take a swim. I hadn't brought a suit with me, and as I stood there, Annie came outside.

"You can borrow one of mine," she said, handing me a one-piece that had been draped on the railing to dry. It was tie-dyed or airbrushed, three neon stripes across its chest.

"I don't think it'll fit," I said. "It looks too small."

"Who cares," Annie said. "It'll work for now." Because they had the baby, Annie and her husband had installed a metal gate around the pool. "Just take your time," she said, as I opened the gate and jumped in. She then walked to the house and picked up the phone, probably calling Howard to talk about *PokerWorld,* which was always on the verge of going under.

After finishing my laps and hanging limply in the water for what seemed like an hour, Annie finally emerged from the kitchen.

"Mind if I join you?" she asked, sitting down. There was Maudie on her hip, her arms waving wildly in the air like flesh propellers.

"She wants her auntie," Annie said. I waded for a moment, then climbed up the ladder. "I don't think I can handle her," I said.

She asked Maudie if she wanted to nurse. Maudie pawed at

her chest. I stared at Annie's breast as she took it from her bra, the veins like tiny wires beneath the skin.

"You want a lesson?" she said. I'd been trying to get her to give me a lesson since the day I'd arrived, but she'd always redirected me to Howard.

I told her that, yes, I would like it if she'd give me a lesson.

"Get the cards."

So I got them.

"You deal."

So I dealt.

"Now this is one-on-one—heads-up."

"Just you and me," I said.

"And the thing about playing just us is position is everything. You're playing your opponent, not the cards—but you know this. And whoever acts first, if they don't take the lead, then you usually raise. So let's see what I've got." She flipped up an ace and a two. "How about you?"

"A jack-nine."

"Now we both have so-so cards, but I have the ace so I'm going to raise unless you raise first."

"But why, when you can just call and take a look at the flop for half the price?"

"Because I'm pretty sure I've got you beat, and you want to get your money in whenever you're the favorite."

When I was much younger, maybe seven years old, my sister and I would play cards fairly often. Though she was twice my age, she must have loved the fact that I was easily bullied, but I didn't perceive this then—I just wanted to play. I would go to her room, pitch my head to one side, swab her face with my sad little eyes. "Can we play a game of cards?" I'd say.

"I suppose," she'd reply, as she got off her bed, settled down on the floor, and leaned menacingly forward. "But you have to deal."

"Yes, I know," I would say, and I'd shuffle the cards, which were bent, sometimes torn—as easy to cheat with as any deck of cards I've ever seen.

Because I was so young, I would ask that Annie play me in the simpler games like Spit and, if we had time, War. If I was feeling really ambitious, I might ask for Go Fish, which was far more complex, a real memory game. Though I'm sure the choice of games must have seemed awfully constricting to my sister, she liked them well enough, liked the slap of the cards on the deck, the elation of winning, which was nearly her prerogative.

I remember one day when we played with my mother and Howard on the family room rug. My brother was kneeling, my mother was sitting on a chair that she'd pulled to the edge of the game. I was leaning my back against the dusty TV, awaiting my chance to play a complicated grown-up game. Annie had taken her usual position, cross-legged and slouching, her bangs hanging over her eyes. We were playing a game I'd never played before called Hearts. It was a game meant for four, like bridge, and because my father wasn't there, my sister had asked if I'd like to fill in, an offer I had greedily accepted.

"Now the way it works is like this. You have the four suits, the hearts are the worst, and you have to follow suit. If you're out of the suit you can discard another suit, including hearts, which is good because for every heart you win, you get a point."

"OK," I said.

"The queen of spades is worth thirteen whole bad points, not good to get." I nodded. "And so the goal is to keep from getting points, to get zero if you can. *Unless* you think you can win *all* the hearts *and* the queen of spades, in which case, you 'shoot the moon,' which means everyone else in the hand will get twenty-six points and you will get *zero*."

"You'll get it," said my mother. "You're old enough for this."

Howard shuffled the cards.

I remember looking hard at the hand I'd been dealt, at the hearts and the queen, which I passed to my left, getting rid of them as quickly as I could. The game was complex, and my sister kept hitting my arm and repeating the rules so I'd act in proper turn. I didn't know what I was doing, but I figured something out: I should *give* my cards away. While my siblings and my mother were trying whenever they could to "shoot the moon," I was playing with the utmost passivity. I was giving every card away, no matter what I held. Never trying to do much of anything else, until by the end of the game I had won. I hadn't taken any risks, you see, but yet I had won.

"You're so passive," said Annie. The lentils were finished. The spinach was steaming on the table in a bowl. We were sitting on the patio. My sister had taken the hand.

"Well, I think that *you're* too aggressive."

Annie laughed. "I'm just playing the way you're supposed to," she said. "Now I want you to raise."

"But I think my cards aren't good enough."

"Well, you're probably reading them wrong. This is heads-up, this isn't nine people at a table, sitting around, sharing an entire deck. Chances are you have the better hand exactly half the time. But it doesn't even matter. Just play *me,*" she said.

I looked at my sister. At her face, which had aged, at her skin, which was loose at her chin. Her face had grown care-worn, from the baby or the poker, from the passage of time—from all three of them combined.

"OK, raise," I replied.

"No, play *me*." She started laughing. "So I've tricked you again."

It was dark. I was growing impatient.

"If we had any chips, you'd have gotten them all by now," I said.

"But we don't have chips and Bennie isn't home and we've got all this time. You just don't like to lose."

"Not to you," I said. "God knows I've lost to you enough as it is."

"But wouldn't you rather lose to me now, with no money, than later if you get to my table?"

"If I get to your table? Do you think I could get to your table?"

"I'm not sure." Annie frowned. "You can read people well. But you seem a little tentative."

"So what should I do?"

"I don't know," Annie said. "In a way, you've really got to be stupid to get up very high. I remember this guy—he sat down at my table just the other night. He was in his mid-twenties, a little bit older than you, and he put down two full racks of hundreds—it was twenty thousand dollars altogether—and I'd never seen him before."

"That seems weird."

"It *was* weird. Highly unusual. And he didn't look like anyone who'd have a lot of money, so I asked him: 'Hey, where are you from?' and he was from just across the room, where he played some lower game, like three- to six-dollar Hold 'Em, where you play. He explained that he'd sold off his jeans in the morning—for ten or twenty dollars—and then played a full day straight, before getting to my table, which wasn't any place he should have been."

"So the guy was no good, but he went on some streak?"

"That's right," Annie said. "And he didn't even have his jeans anymore. He was wearing these old, worn-out khakis, and he was sitting there across from me at the table, looking lost."

"Shouldn't he have known better?" I asked. "Shouldn't he have taken all those hundred-dollar chips and put them on a car or on a house?"

"But that's not how things work," Annie said. "For the guy to have amassed the twenty thousand dollars in the first place means he was a maniac. People just aren't rational."

"So what happened?"

"So this guy was now across from me, and he's staring, and he must be on something or other, and the dealer deals me perfect eights, I get rolled up with eights." (In Stud, "rolled up" means that the first three cards a player's dealt make trips.) "I have these great trips, but the guy can see only the one eight that's showing, so I play him for all he's worth, and he loses twenty thousand dollars then and there. And I wouldn't say I felt bad, because that's just not how I felt, but it wasn't a pleasant thing to take money from such a clueless person. And I just can't see you being happy having to make that decision again and again, like Howard and I have to do—to take someone's money, even if they do happen to be a total *moron*."

14 ♠ Expectations

Though I remember many days that I spent in Las Vegas, the nights I recall only vaguely. Session after session playing cards at my low-limit table, lost to memory. I played with great fervor—I remember that—and waking to the rustling of leaves, the skin around my eyes as dark as coffee rings. At dusk I would go to play poker again, mechanically shifting the gears of the car, darting from corner to corner till I reached the Mirage. It was a gleaming, incredibly beautiful building, bright and sublime as a new bar of gold, and I loved walking slowly through its glass double doors, toward the room where my sister and brother played cards. Was I there to learn poker or to feel like a part of the family? I guess both.

Those early hands lost, though I wrote them all down on a small pad of paper that I'd filched from the card room. The other players would look on in amusement at the terribly serious girl who wrote down their plays: "Man in first position: raise. *His right hand is shaking.* Woman to his right: call. Ninth seat: reraise. First seat: call. Call. Flop comes 8–3–6, different suits. Check, then bet. Raise. *Woman's jugular pulsing.* Call. Call. Ace of spades. Bet. *Man's hand still shaking.* Call. Ninth seat folds. (Man must have an ace?) Final card comes: Jack. Bet. Woman hesitates. *Covers her mouth with her hand.* Call." After checking my opinions with Howard at dinner, I would stuff the notes in a clear plastic binder. All those notes, all those hands. Even if I'd kept them, I wouldn't now remember the way those hands played out, the way, for example, the woman's head listed when she brandished her ace-king of hearts. Or the way that the first seat had tilted his hat while his right hand, *still shaking,* had thrown in his cards.

"And what do you think happened there?" Howard asked after hearing me narrate this hand.

"I think the first seat also had an ace, but his second card was smaller."

"I think you're exactly right," Howard said. "Nice job. Now when are you going to stop with the notes and just remember?"

"I don't know," I said, picking at the lukewarm baked potato on my plate. "I don't know if I'll ever be able to remember. All the hands just bleed into one another, you know? And all the people."

"No, I don't know," said Howard. "You can't just spend your whole life taking notes while you play. I know they must *feel* real, but they're not real."

All my life it had struck me that my sister and brother had better memories than I. When I was much younger, I would notice how easily and quickly they'd study for their tests, how well they could learn any fact or statistic. I'd always assumed that this uncanny ability had come from my mother, who, my father would regularly remind us, used to borrow his notes back in graduate school, memorize them in a single sitting, then proceed to do better on the test than he. My father just loved to extol my mother's knack for rote memorization (a knack that had helped her through the years with all her plays), yet even then, when I was young, I doubted the value of this particular variety of photographic memory. It seemed like a cheat.

Not that I wasn't impressed. I can remember listening to Annie and Howard as they'd talk about cards. They could narrate almost any hand exactly as it had happened, even those hands that had happened several years before, and in such a thick and impenetrable jargon that I'd have trouble just following along. I knew I didn't have that kind of talent, but I also knew that a player could be very good without it, so I didn't despair. Besides, I had my own equally inane type of photographic memory: for colors, for scenes, for the way that people said things. This more visceral way of remembering the past meant that I was able to "read" people well, but it proved problematic. I would sit at my table, look around at my opponents, and try my best to assess them by their postures and expressions, but it would be strangely painful. Or, not painful. It would make me feel *dirty*. A poker table is one of the only places in the world where people are encouraged to downright stare at one another. A player's entire body becomes part of the game, an extension of the cards—in fact a stand-in for the cards—and so I'd stare. I'd stare and they'd stare, and then I'd become uncomfortable at staring, at watching the other players staring. Their faces would grow tired, ashen, their expressions severe. We would sit there, growing filthy together, handling our cards and the dirty plastic chips, trying not to bite our nails for fear of what had lodged itself beneath them.

The cardinal sin in poker, worse than playing dud cards, worse even than figuring your odds incorrectly, is becoming emotionally involved. While the game requires that you fully engage with other players at the table, that you pay attention to their quirks and personalities, you're not supposed to identify with them in any way. You are, in other words, expected to empathize with your opponents while remaining devoid of all compassion. It is very hard to do.

While my sister and brother would remember their hands with a mechanical precision, their opponents merely actors, nothing more, I'd remember mine in such a sensory fashion that I'd often lose the logic of the hand as it had happened, and when I stopped taking notes, I felt suddenly unmoored. It was exposing to sit there, no pencil to keep my hands busy. I was just this little girl, I'd think, *a child,* though by then I was twenty-two. The other players at my table would regularly pity me, advising me to fold when they knew they had me beat, refraining from raising in spite of the fact that they'd read my poor odds in my face. In this way, I gained an advantage by being a woman in Vegas, an advantage that, in and of itself, may have accounted for my tiny $2-an-hour edge. I knew it couldn't last, however, and one day—it was very bad timing, I had just quit the *PokerWorld* job—I met up with a man with no pitying bone in his body.

Mealy Joe was an elderly man, maybe sixty years old. His skin resembled oatmeal, a yellow sort of brown, pocked on his cheeks and his neck by old acne scars, and this is why I called him Mealy Joe. I could never figure out why Joe played low. His skills at the table were, if not flawless, then at least profitable, and he should have moved up long before. From the bits of conversation I'd overheard him engaging in that night, I gleaned that he'd been in the navy at some point, stuck on some long band of blue, waiting for orders that took a few months to arrive. "Nothin' to do but play cards," he grumbled. "All the day and all the night. The best time of my life I had on that boat."

By the time I was seated, Joe had already drained a good deal of the money from the table. His stack was as wide and as tall as a bread box, and his face, which was normally sallow, was flushed. The other players at the table had not simply been unlucky; to a one they were terrible. In poker parlance, they would be deemed "calling stations," which means they were willing to play almost any hand, no matter how much of an underdog to win, and call it all the way to the end just to see how things turned out. They never raised, but they hardly ever folded, and this made it difficult to know what they were holding. My way of dealing with this problem was to sit on my hands until I held premium cards, cards that I felt would beat anything. A more experienced player like Mealy Joe, however, had another way of playing such a table. He would check-raise and bluster his way to big pots, playing hands that he knew were unbeatable weakly, and soaking up the action like a sponge. When he didn't have much, he would wait till the end, observing the other players' postures. If it looked as if they hadn't hit (something he could ascertain in an instant, he was that good), he'd raise—and they'd fold.

After watching Mealy Joe dominate the table in this way for some hours, and after playing just a couple of hands myself, I was dealt a king-queen of different suits in the sixth position, which means that I was right in the middle of the order of play. Everyone after the second seat had folded, and so, in large part to bully the remaining players out of the pot, I raised.

The player in the eight-seat called, but all the other players folded. I thought I was home free, but when it came to Mealy Joe, who was waiting rather slyly in the first seat for the action, he raised.

"You're not getting away with anything tonight, little miss," he said, crossing and uncrossing his slim sailor's legs. "I call your three dollars and I raise you three more."

I reraised.

The eight-seat folded.

"I'll call you," said Joe, his face cracking open in a rictus. "I guess it's you and me, young miss. Alone."

I remember my cheeks welling up with blood—and the tremor in my hands and wrists. Mealy Joe was smart enough to know that this could mean anything. Maybe I was sitting on a strong pair of cards. Or maybe I had nothing. Whatever I was holding, I was terrified—terrified of Mealy Joe. Terrified of losing.

But then the flop came: two queens and an ace, three different suits. I now had three queens and a king, a strong hand, a hand almost nothing could beat, but Joe bet into me. He didn't even hesitate. I raised. But then he raised me back. We capped it. (Did he have the other queen? I wasn't any good at reading Joe.)

The dealer dealt a jack of hearts, then neatened up the cards:

Q♥ Q♠ A♦ J♥

The action was with Mealy Joe. He bet. "Sure are a lot of face cards on the table," he said.

"No shit," I said. "Raise."

He reraised. I called. The dealer called, "King." (Did Joe have a king? An ace-king? I was thinking too much, and my hands were still shaking.)

"What do you have?" I asked.

"That's for me to know and you to find out," he replied. There was no single trace of trepidation in his voice, but I had a full house, so I raised.

We capped the bets.

"Show your cards," said the dealer. I turned my hand over.

"I have queens full of kings," I said, choking back something. (Not tears, it was drier than that.)

"Well, what d'ya know?" said Mealy Joe. "I got myself a full house too. I got myself *trip-aces and two queens.*"

• • •

But why was I there? Why *really*? It's a question I ask myself often enough, even from here, some years later: New York—even from here, in this book. And I suppose that the answer's fairly simple to figure, though I doubt I was aware of it back then. I had come to Las Vegas to trade something in—to trade in my family, which had broken up unhappily when I had been a girl, for this new one, which had reconvened out here in such a giddy place. I had come to Las Vegas to reacquaint myself with strangers. But it wasn't as simple as that.

There was, first of all, the matter of our distance from each other. While I lived in Las Vegas, I hardly ever saw all three of them together—my mother and my sister and brother—let alone my father. They were living separate lives by then, and though I'd sometimes catch my siblings sitting next to one another playing poker, or see a movie with my mother or my brother late at night, we weren't quite a family. It was different. We were more like friends. Or maybe just business associates.

Second, as anyone knows, when you go to Las Vegas to trade something in, you usually leave with far less than you'd hoped for, if you leave with much of anything at all. It's an economy of loss, not gain, though the blinking casinos would seem to claim the opposite. I had come to Las Vegas to trade myself in, but I didn't leave Vegas with the self I'd expected. Yes, I got to learn poker from my siblings, and I got to spend time with my mother, a person I hadn't known well in my youth, but these were different people now. I too was very different, and geographical proximity could never change those facts.

Finally, of course, I had come to learn poker, but by the time I quit at *PokerWorld*, I wasn't very good. I was breaking even, maybe even winning a little overall. My hourly expectation had risen to $3 an hour. (The most that a player can reasonably expect to make in an hour is dependent on both her play and the stakes of the game; in my $3–$6 Hold 'Em game, for instance, $6 an hour is going to be the maximum expectation for most players. Similarly, in the $300–$600 Hold 'Em game that my siblings were playing in, $600 would be the maximum hourly expectation.) I was better than I had been, but I wasn't yet ready to play any higher, a fact that made me feel ashamed. My sister and brother were by this time world-class players, and I lived in great fear of becoming an appendage—their little sister who could write but who was not so great at cards.

Because the good majority of the poker players had gotten into the business on a lark or out of desperation, none of them could understand why I, who had a fine B.A., would ever have gone in for poker, regardless of my lineage. One player, Godfrey, who was carrot-topped and portly, grabbed me by the elbow one night and refused to let me go until I listened to his rant.

"You went to college, right?"

"That's right."

"Then what the fuck are you doing here?"

"I don't know what you're talking about."

"Don't give me that crap. I know who you are."

"I'm nobody."

"No—no, you're somebody. And speaking as a real nobody to a real somebody, you're an idiot to be here at all."

"Godfrey," I said. "It's me. I'm not an asshole."

"No, you're not an asshole, but I'm an asshole."

"You're not an asshole," I muttered.

"You think it's fun? You think it's anything other than a grind, to sit here, for hours, playing the same stupid cards, the same cards the same ways? Making the same stupid plays?"

I tried to extricate myself, but his fingers were pressing.

"Get out before you find yourself like me: overweight, with earphones glued to your head; sick and pale and fucking impotent."

"OK!" I said, and he let me go.

Even some of the higher-limit players had told me to leave. Erik had told me to focus on my writing. "You can make something better than this," he said. "Money's not that important." Though I felt there was something beautiful to poker and that the things I learned while playing the game were of significant value and worth, I could see where the lifestyle would drive a person crazy. There was the playing till all hours of the night, for one, and the huge fluctuations in luck, which battered the self-esteem. I doubted I'd be able to take it. I wanted so badly to make an easy living, however, that I kept on with the playing—in spite of the fact that my hands would be shaking, in spite of the clackety-clacking of chips, the long sitting for hours and my back knitting up like a boot.

I would go back to Z's, loaf around, bend and stretch. I would sit at the very clean, very clear desk in the room with the broken TV. I would sit there and write—write a poem, a review—whatever I could get my worn-out head to try to do. I would sometimes attempt to describe all those things that I'd seen at the tables: the nasty Greek shipping magnate, who'd play with my brother and sister for weeks at a clip, losing millions, his brow like a patch on his forehead. Or I'd write about the Warlock Man, with his flowing white hair, sulfur mustache, and venal expression. One night he had offered to give me some lessons, and had even invited me back to his house near Lake Mead, which was furnished with a small black settee, tall black chairs, a black table in which I could see my reflection, my face floating within it as if in a dark water. I'd accepted the offer in spite of the fact both my siblings had told me the man couldn't play.

"He's a hack."

"You're so judgmental."

"He doesn't know a thing."

"But he's so *interesting*."

"He's really just a dumb cliché. If you're thinking that you'll write about him later, remember that he's just a dumb cliché."

A dumb cliché. I suppose they were right, though a great writer—Fitzgerald or Wharton—a truly great writer about money could have found originality in all of that cliché, could have found the ticking truth behind the faces and the chips. I, however, could not. It all retained the feel of sheen, and I gave up rather quickly—not only on attempting to describe all the gamblers, but also on seeing my way through their manners and means. With or without the notes, I couldn't seem to empathize.

I played with Mealy Joe only one other time. My father was in town. He was staying with me in Z's mansion, and I'd drive him around, showing him sights that neither of us cared for much but that both of us believed it was our duty to take in: the great, grinning sphinx crouched in front of the Luxor; the volcano that erupted on the hour at the Mirage; all the tourists who walked down the street, their feet shuffling exhaustedly along.

One night, after driving back and forth in this fashion, I'd insisted that my father watch me play a little poker, a demand to which he acquiesced, if not enthusiastically then at least cordially. Looking back now, I can see that I was jealous, jealous of my sister and my brother for their giant stakes, jealous of the fact that they'd redeemed the family's unremarkable impoverishment.

When we got to the poker room, I was dismayed to see that the only available seat was next to Mealy Joe. I sat down and put my chips on the table, the two of us warily eyeing each other.

Though I cannot remember the hands that were played, I can vividly remember stealing glances at my father, who was sitting right behind me. I explained every move I made to him with excessive pride. I played a lot of hands that night that I had no business playing, just to keep him entertained. There is an old saying that watching a person play poker is just about as interesting as watching paint dry, and I was worried he was bored. He kept leaning over, putting his hands in the shape of a steeple, putting the point of the steeple to his chin, resting his face on the steeple.

"Are you bored?" I asked.

"No," he said. "I'm having . . . I'm having a *wonderful* time."

"Because if you're bored we can go. Or maybe Annie and Howard will get here and play. We can watch them play?"

"No, no."

But he was clearly bored.

And then Mealy Joe, who kept looking and looking. I managed to win a small pot from him then, but otherwise we didn't play (ever again, for that matter).

In my mind, I suppose, I will always associate my father with old Mealy Joe, their boredom, their amusement at watching me play.

15 ♠ A Girl's Room

One night, after losing all my money, I drove to my mother's east side house. I would often stop over at her place after playing, and on this night in particular I was greedy for companionship.

"I didn't hear you come in," she said, sitting up on the couch. "How'd it go?"

"Not so well," I said, slumping. "I lost over two hundred dollars."

"If it makes you feel any better," she replied, "Howard and Z got killed on football last night. I don't know what the hell happened."

As I stood there at a loss for what to say, she pushed off her blanket and walked toward the kitchen. She sat at her desk, which was covered in papers, and it made for a sense of déjà vu. The nightie was the same (she got a new one every Christmas); the hair-style was the same (the short-cropped cut was what framed her features best); and her voice, it was strangely the same (a luxurious rasp; she had smoked a pack a day for thirty years).

"Come here by me," she said, sitting down on a wooden high-backed chair. "I could use some company, if you're not too exhausted."

She'd made a mistake with the figures for the day. When she'd tallied the action, it had come out to one hundred thousand too much.

"There's got to be some extra zeros in here, and I have no idea how to find them without doing the entire set of figures again." She handed me a fresh sheet of paper. "Will you do me a favor and just fill in the names while I warm up my coffee?"

"Sure," I said, taking hold of the sheet. As I went through the names (Gollum, Atilla, Maniac), I listened as my mother pressed the buttons on the microwave. Her manicured nails made a gentle clicking sound as they hit the display and I couldn't help but wonder how such a coddled, if ultimately befuddled, creature had ended up working for her sports-betting son.

By the time I arrived in Las Vegas, I'd applied to a number of creative writing programs, and for the months I spent learning poker, I was waiting to hear whether or not I'd been accepted. On those nights when I didn't play cards, I would go to my mother's with a sheaf of my poems and ask her to critique them.

She was a marvelous reader, surprisingly so, since she didn't read poetry often. She had a natural sense of rhythm, and had been passionate about the poetry of Yeats when she'd been young. She'd also quite admired Wallace Stevens, or so I ascertained, seeing as she'd refer to him whenever she'd critique my work.

"It's like Stevens," she would say. "The way you use the

words and skip the meaning. But the music has to work, the syntax. The meaning *is* the syntax." She would read the poem slowly, then quickly. She would read it to herself and then out loud. She would purse her lips and cross her legs, her nightie bunching up around her hips.

After she'd finished with her figures for the evening and found out where the mutinous zeros had been hiding, she sat down on the luminous couch and lit a Merit. She asked if I'd brought any poems.

"No," I said. "I haven't written in a while." She puffed and she puffed as she stared at the pool. I imagined this her form of meditation—staring pensively out at the clear lapping water, the moon like a brilliant idea in the sky.

"Well," she said, "I hope you get into one of those schools. Poker is going to ruin you. I really believe that.

"I mean," she continued bitterly, "I went to New York to do the acting, which I just loved—you know how much I loved it. And now I'm in this horrid city where the traffic lights are so long and there isn't even a decent art museum. What the hell happened to the acting? It was the money, that's what it was. Money can't be that important."

I nodded my head.

"And I know it must have seemed like it was terribly important, the way your father and I fought about it when you were little. But it isn't. You can get along if you're happy." She paused. "You know what makes me happy is reading this book." She picked up a volume from the coffee table and handed it to me. "It's this book about Native Americans. The author's reconstructed how they lived, you know, like in those *Clan of the Cave Bear* books, and it's so wonderful and true and I believe it completely. I have only five pages left and I don't want it to end."

I flipped through the pages.

"I wish I could write a book like that," she said. "I've had an interesting life—I really have—and I think to myself, 'I'm going to die, and it will be like I never existed' and if I'd only gotten up, gotten out of my nightie, and if I'd only thought about things just a little, I might have written something good." She paused. "But you know what I really wanted to be, much more than I ever wanted to be a writer, was an archaeologist. I always wanted to go to Egypt and dig up bones and sit in the sun with a shovel in my hand and just think and look at statues and run my hands along the old walls, because you know how I like to sit in the sun. But my mother made me major in economics."

"Yes, I know," I said.

"She said I had to study something 'practical.' But these days, if I'd studied Latin and archaeology like I'd wanted to, I could be off on some dig, not in Vegas just some glorified accountant."

Whatever she might have thought about herself, my mother was much more than just a glorified accountant. She did the numbers for a high-stakes gambling operation in Las Vegas, where all three of her children now lived and played poker, but she somehow never saw herself as anyone peculiar. She was simply a mother who happened to work for her son, just as any other mother might have done. And, in a way, she had a point. I remember all those nights, all those times I'd see her sitting there, in the den, in her nightie, doing figures, playing solitaire. Nothing much had really changed. I remember when I was quite young, walking in on her doing her puzzles, which she'd stack in her little kitchen nook. She had a number of colorful books, specialty dictionaries, and these I'd peruse when she wasn't around, hoisting myself onto her unsteady chair, rifling through all the things on her desk: the brass urn-shaped ashtray, the pens, which were inkless and dull, all the diadems of domestic life, a little overused, a little ruined.

And in my head I had simply transposed her from that little kitchen nook back home in my youth to the new one here in Vegas. Whereas the old one was sullied, stained with fingerprints and coffee rings, this one was made of a bright cherry wood. There was a fax machine, a telephone, expensive, gushing pens. All through the night she would add up those figures, pressing the nub of her pencil to the buttons of the adding machine, which would make a horrid cranking sound—not so much a *cha-ching* as a *CCHHH-CCHHH-CCHHH-CCHHH*. And then in the daytime, she'd go to the office and place Howard's bets, though I hardly ever saw her there. I think in a way I didn't *want* to see her there, and I never did set foot in the office during working hours. Indeed, I saw the office only once and even then late at night, with no one there.

Howard was taking us out to dinner, and the three of us had piled into his Lexus to go. He had a favorite restaurant, a Thai place called Komol, which served rich spicy food and cold water in squat amber glasses. It was right near the office, and he figured he'd stop there and pick up some keys. Though his betting operation was technically legal in Nevada, this didn't mean it was welcome, and I, for one, was nervous at the thought of stopping by. I had never seen one of the betting offices before, and I'd always imagined them to look chaotic, like the office my mother had described back in New York.

From the outside, the building where the office was housed looked drab. It was located in that particular part of Las Vegas that's neither here nor there—not the Strip, not the suburbs, not even the place where the pawn shops and wedding chapels cluster. Inside, however, the place was surprisingly well appointed. In the center of the room sat two fluffy couches, each big enough to accommodate four very large behinds. To the right, near a small, narrow kitchen, was a tiny, round table stacked with ransacked, crumpled bags of chips. Two TVs hung from the ceiling like household gods, and as I looked around the office, taking in the newfangled accoutrements, I couldn't help but wonder how it differed from a stock brokerage firm. The principles of both were the same: buy low, sell high; keep a diversified portfolio; never bet more than you can afford to lose; and, finally, if you ever find you're in too deep, reduce your positions. Of course, there was a major and rather glaring difference between a stock brokerage firm and a sports betting business: one was considered completely legit while the other crossed a blurry legal line. And so, even then, with all the money flowing in, I knew that at any moment it might end.

• • •

It must have been four in the morning when I finally went to bed. I remember the ripples of light in the sky and the moon falling low on the horizon. My mother was asleep on the couch, and though she'd brought a blanket out with her, I didn't think it right to leave her sleeping in the cold.

"Mother," I said, tapping on her shoulder. "It's time to go."

She rubbed her eyes. "What time is it? When did I fall asleep? Let me get you to bed."

In a kind of garret at the top of the stairs was a very large, white bed where I slept when I stayed at my mother's. It functioned as a centerpiece around which she'd arrayed a set of antique wicker furniture. There was a chair with a little blue pillow and a small, long-legged table. There was also a perambulator with wheels—presumably an homage to little Maud. On the walls, which were papered in pink and beige, illegible epitaphs were printed, scripted in a dainty cursive hand. All in all, the room looked as if it belonged to a girl so prim and small that she'd have tremendous difficulty in ascending the giant white bed by herself.

"That's why I bought the little footstool," my mother said, pushing it under my feet so I could get into bed without having to jump. "I had quite a time finding it—I had to go to Bed Bath & Beyond—and you know I hate to drive—and I had never been to that store before, even though it was right around the corner, and it must have taken me three hours to find the stool. Oh, God, it was awful."

It had always been a peculiar characteristic of my mother that she hardly went out. I suppose she'd be called a recluse, though when I was very young, I didn't know such a word existed and assumed she was simply afraid to face the world when she was drunk. Once she'd gotten sober, however, she continued to shut herself in, settling down after her work in an unctuous cloud of smoke. I can remember when she'd lived in New York she would order all her dinners in, eating from a tinfoil dish that she'd set on the floor for her cats. In Vegas, the problem had been further compounded. For Vegas, unlike New York, is a city dominated by cars, and it's not only possible, but even probable, for a person to spend all their time indoors—in their houses or in the casinos—venturing out only to take out the garbage.

"I mean, I get back from that office, and I'm just exhausted. And then I have to stay up all night and do the figures, and there's just no energy left anymore. . . ."

"So why don't you quit doing figures and play cards?" I asked. Howard and Annie had been trying to get her to play poker for years. She was brilliant at bridge and brilliant at cards in general; why wouldn't she be a great poker player? The two of them would back her and they'd make a lot of money. That was their plan.

"I don't like the idea of playing cards for money," she replied, scrunching up her nose. "I can do numbers for Howard in my nightie at my desk. To play poker, I'd have to get dressed up and drive over to the casino. And besides, I don't like to look at people's faces when they lose."

"But either way you'd be doing something risky," I said. "You know you're going to look like bookies no matter what you do and who knows if the next time they'll put you in jail? I mean, even in Vegas, they don't really like a bookie. No one likes a bookie. Doesn't that bother you?"

"I don't know."

"But you do know. You know it's risky. It's *gambling*."

"You don't approve?" She looked surprised.

"No, I . . ."

"Ah, but you've *never* approved," she sighed.

I told her that it wasn't true. That I wasn't trying to attack her.

"But I think that's precisely what you're trying to do," she replied. "And I know it's not completely right. What do you want me to say?"

"I just want you to admit that you're reckless. That you've always been reckless." (I *was* trying to attack her.) "You sit here in your beautiful house and watch TV, and then, in the daytime, you go out and gamble."

"But I need to make a living. What else do you want me to do? You gamble too, you know. *Everybody* gambles, and if you or society wants to put me in jail for it, then go ahead and stop taking so goddamned long."

16 Façades

That autumn, I abandoned both Las Vegas and my poker career to enroll in the poetry program at the University of Iowa. It was a jarring move, from hot desert wastes to corn-addled farmlands, but I welcomed it. I'd grown tired of all the late nights playing poker—and of not having money. I had also grown tired of the players. The students in the program were eccentric, even difficult, but their manners were reassuringly familiar, and when I first arrived there, on that midwestern campus, I felt relieved. Even though I'd started writing poetry for grades, it had become something else in my life. It had become the most important thing.

In spite of the fact that I was thrilled to be seriously writing again, that first autumn in the program moved glacially slowly. I arrived with no friends, and the nature of the program, which funded its students unequally, infused our interactions with suspicion and a mutual contempt. I remember the first afternoon that the rosters for the workshops were posted. A slight girl I'd met just that morning had accompanied me over to the bulletin board. When she saw that I'd been chosen for the section she'd requested, she threw me a sharp, dirty look and hardly ever spoke to me again. Though I would have once relished beating someone so readily out of a spot, it didn't feel good anymore. I was tired of competition.

In order to improve my poems, which were wildly uneven, I'd go to a café downtown and guzzle cups of coffee. I'd sit, waiting blankly for a friend or aquaintance to appear, chat a little, crack some jokes. The program was highly unstructured, and we had a great deal of time. There was a genial square through which students would mull, and I'd wander outside, and forget all the things that depressed me.

But then one cold day in early December, a day far too cold to be walking outside, I heard about the bust. I'm not sure if I read about it first, or if a member of the family called, but the newspaper said that my brother was in jail. The Las Vegas police had raided his offices, believing he was part of a $400-million-a-year illegal sports betting network with strong ties to organized crime.

The police had apparently been planning the raid for some time, casing the office, my brother, and my mother. And one day they came and just turned the place over.

My mother hadn't been there. "Luckily they didn't come and get me," she said when she called me on the phone a few days later. "You have no idea how lucky that was. It meant that I didn't have to be handcuffed to some horrible person the way your brother was, and forced to play mind chess with the heroin addicts all around in the dirty cell. But they did come to my house to search. I couldn't believe it—I still can't believe it. And they knocked on the door with these very big guns, and of course I let them in, but it almost seemed like they wanted to break the door down, they were so gruff. And one of them—there were three altogether—one walked over and frisked me. All up and down, and he stopped his hands at my waist and I said, 'Oh, it's just fat under there, officer. I don't have a gun,' but I figured they had to take something, so I went into the office and handed them the figures for the week. I also had twenty-five hundred dollars in Christmas money in my underwear drawer, and I didn't want them finding that because then I wouldn't be able to afford to buy presents this year, and so I tried to be cooperative."

"Are you going to jail?" I interrupted. "Did they find things in the office that would put you in jail?"

"I don't know," said my mother. "I don't know if we're going to jail. Your brother's out for now, thank God. But the whole thing's caught up in court and with all the new laws they can keep all our money for a really long time."

In addition to raiding the office and my mother's stucco Tudor, they'd confiscated Howard's box of chips at the Mirage. His bank accounts were frozen, and he had to borrow money from his friends to pay his mortgage.

"He won't be playing poker for a while," said my mother. "But the thing was I had this Christmas money and I was so worried they were going to find it. They looked around in the den. They had a tech guy come in and look over my computer. 'All she does is play games,' he said, so they let me keep that."

"There wasn't anything else to find?"

"No, nothing but those figures, which I gave him, I mean, I

was happy to hand them over—and the Christmas money. I just don't know, I guess they weren't that bright, because they never even looked in my underwear drawer. And I was nervous, really scared, you know—I tried to feed the cats out on the porch while I was waiting for them to search around, and one of the officers completely freaked out. He thought that there was money in the cat food . . . so I didn't do that again.

"And so I went into my room and took the money from the drawer and said, 'Officer, this is my Christmas money, can I please keep it?' And he nodded and said that I could."

Because of the bust, my brother and Z had to shut down their offices for good. They were never officially tried, but in order to keep themselves out of the courts, they were forced to pay a hefty fine that put them out of business. Though the two of them missed all the income they'd gotten from their years of betting sports, it was my mother who suffered most. She was out of a job, broke, and it was unclear whether or not she would be able to keep her house. After two weeks of painful uncertainty, she found a job working for a bettor named Sugey, but he wasn't nearly as kind to my mother as my brother had been, and she was miserable working double the hours for only half the pay. She began to think seriously about moving away from Las Vegas.

In order to figure out what he should do, Howard went on a golfing vacation to Arizona that summer, and he asked me to stay in his house and take care of his dogs. Because I was in writing school, without a full-time job, I had no money to speak of, and house-sitting for my brother seemed as good a way as any to pass the summer without having to work.

• • •

Howard's house at this time (and the house I always think of when I imagine him in Vegas, though he finally had to sell) was located in a master-planned community called Summerlin, which had been growing like a cancer through the Las Vegas Valley. It sprawled across the valley floor, from the vicinity of Rainbow all the way to Red Rock Canyon, and was a perplexity to the mind. Even though the housing was designed to appeal to the wealthy, and even though a significant portion of the city's lawyers, doctors, executives, and chefs lived within its gated communities, the place amounted to a fancy trailer park—tract housing for the rich. All of the domiciles resembled one another to such a degree that it was easy to get lost just going to the market and I would find myself disoriented among the endless rows of identical houses, driving from cul-de-sac to cul-de-sac in circles, kids on Big Wheels pedaling past, Mexican grounds-men everywhere, watering the lawns with their wilted plastic hoses, the gates behind me opening and closing, a panic bracing my entire body so that I'd break into frustrated tears before finally discovering the house.

Howard had purchased a lot in a particular subdivision called the Enclave, which was next to a lot owned by the tennis star Andre Agassi and his girlfriend at the time, Brooke Shields. In order to oversee the building of his dream house, Howard had purchased a smaller, prefabricated place a block away, which was where I stayed that summer. Although it wasn't as fancy as the houses in the Enclave, this house was quite luxurious, two ample stories high, with an expansive backyard that was landscaped by a pair of dwarfish gardeners. They would appear and disappear as if by some weird magic, leaving trails of red and purple flowers in their wake. The yard was just outside the living room, which was grand and full of light, and I can remember spending long afternoons watching the wide-screened TV or just listening to music. An alarm system kept track of any movement in the house, and I had to take great pains not to set it off by accident. Sometimes the dogs would trip the lasers and a robotic-sounding woman would call me on the telephone and ask if everything was OK, in response to which I'd give a hearty laugh, trying to make it all seem just part of the fun, the fun of having money, the fun of being *so safe.* Perhaps the most discomfiting amenity was the automated sprinkler system, which would go off at all hours of the day, its whirring like the sound of hungry locusts.

August was dead as far as poker was concerned. Just as New York psychiatrists go to the Hamptons for the summer, professional poker players go off to Maine or Montana to relax and escape the ruthless heat. It's difficult to convey to a person who hasn't spent any time in Las Vegas how hot it really is. You can feel it on your scalp and palms, on your collarbone and shoulder blades. The sweat streams down your abdomen. Your throat goes dry, your eyelids burn, your entire body is prone, and there's nowhere to go but indoors, where the shades can be drawn and the AC set on high. People in Las Vegas seem never to leave their houses in the summer, and it can be a strange experience to drive along the walkways or past the ubiquitous municipal parks and see no one, as if the place had been deserted long ago. For people from the East, like me, who try to spend whatever time they can outdoors, the apparent abandonment of all outdoor facilities—the sheer emptiness of that part of Las Vegas that sprawls out past the Strip—is a haunting sight, and for the month I spent that summer, sitting for my brother's house, I felt an immense isolation, the kind that makes you wonder if there's really any point to life.

After weeks of unbearable solitude and heat, I received a call from two friends from St. Paul's who wanted to visit on their way to L.A. One, a woman named Sally, was tall with dark hair and a pasty-pale face that had always reminded me of those sketches that fashion designers do—the clothing drawn up in meticulous detail, the countenance merely a smudge. I had known her only vaguely. She'd been part of a well-to-do social circle that I'd joined rather late, and it had always seemed to me that she never much liked it that I hung around. I suspect this was because she herself felt out of place. A native of China, where her father was a diplomat, she was brilliant (I remember hearing her give a report in ninth grade in which she used the word *ponder,* and I was envious) and pretty (with washed-out blue eyes and delicate, coral-pink lips) but a little unsure of herself, a trait that could lead her at times to be cruel.

John, the other friend, was likewise disposed to cruelty, though his breeding was impeccable (he was a blueblood from Boston). It had always been speculated that his father had lost all his money on some business deal, and, presumably because of this, he came off as a little proud.

I remember the surprised expressions on John's and Sally's faces when they finally arrived at the house. It wasn't so much that they hadn't seen many similar houses before—they were, after all, on their way to L.A.—as that they were shocked that a gambler could afford to maintain such a place.

"Is that really all your brother does?" Sally asked with surprise in her voice. "I mean, he just gambles?" I nodded my head, neglecting to tell her the entire operation was falling to pieces.

"He just gambles. He plays poker and bets on sports. That's it. That's what he does."

"Huh," she grunted as she strolled around the living room, running her fingers along the bright spines of the books that lined the far wall, making comments on the titles ("So literary," she said. "*Ulysses.* Has he read it?" "I don't think so. No, not that.") and in general taking stock of all she saw.

"This place is *immense,*" said John, flopping his khaki-clad body on the dark maroon couch. "Maybe we should *all* become gamblers. What do you say, Sally?"

"Seems like a reasonable idea to me, John. I mean, what else could we do? Go to *law school*?" The two of them started to giggle.

I told them that it wasn't that simple, that thousands upon thousands of people made good livings as lawyers, but that only a tiny handful of gamblers made enough to live comfortably. "It's a zero-sum game," I said. "For one person to win enough to live on, there have to be at least five or six losers. That's how it works."

"Well, however it works, your brother's got a cool place." Sally walked out into the yard and John and I followed. "It's so hard to believe that someone can play cards and end up with a pool like this." She took off her shoes, dipped her toes in the water.

"I can turn on some music if you like," I said. "There are speakers in the rocks, see?" I pointed toward some shrubs on the far side of the pool.

"Those aren't real?"

"No—no they're not," I replied, running back into the house. "And there's a waterfall, too. . . ." I said, fiddling with a console on the wall inside the door.

"I'm going to go put on a suit," said John, rummaging through his bags, which he'd left in the foyer and which the dogs were now sniffing. "Get off, poochies!" he said, punting them out of the way.

Once the three of us were safely in the pool, the sun blazing red through the dense valley smog, I couldn't help but wonder: Had my family been right about money all along? Was money all it took to turn a scalding summer day into something so perfectly lovely?

"We should swim around for a while and then go to the Mirage later," I said. "I have some comps for the buffet."

"I was just thinking about dinner," said Sally, paddling around in the shallow end of the pool (John had long ago shimmied over to the deep end, where he continued to somersault and somersault, gasping for air when his face hit the surface). "What a nice afternoon we're having," she continued. "I can't wait to see the Mirage."

It is difficult for a person who has lived under circumstances that are out of the ordinary to remember what it is to live less strangely, but after spending the evening with Sally and John, wandering the blackjack pits, and shopping at the haute couture boutiques, I began to remember the way I'd felt when I'd first come to Vegas—how much I had *seen*. In the years that had intervened since the first time I'd been there, it had receded in my mind, and I no longer registered the strippers or the hookers or the tacky neon signs. My Vegas was no longer the regular Vegas, the Vegas that everyone sees when they visit, that John and Sally saw, the Vegas of mobsters, of Bugsy Siegel. When you're a real person living in Las Vegas, it grows to seem just like any other city, your family just like any other family.

The next morning, John and Sally took advantage of the exercise equipment in the gym my brother had assembled in a room at the front of the house. There was a stationary bike, a StairMaster, a full set of weights, and a treadmill I'd jog on for hours at a time. The room itself was cool and dark, the wood-slatted blinds always perfectly drawn, the speakers embedded in the ceilings and walls.

"I did some laps when I woke up this morning," Sally said. "I feel great."

I looked out at the patio, which was now the scalding white of noon.

"It is nice to swim in the heat, isn't it?" I remarked. I was sitting in the living room, in front of all the dog-eared books, the wide-screen TV, the marble-topped counters, the swirling Persian rug, and, above all, the overbred poochies.

"It really was nice of you to let us stay," Sally went on, drying her hair off with a green cotton towel. She sat down on the love seat. "I've felt so comfortable here. In the buffet last night, at the slots. No one bothers you. No one even looks at you."

I nodded my head.

"You could jump up and down with an aardvark on your head and no one would look at you twice." I remember thinking Sally was exactly right. In Las Vegas you could be the biggest freak of all and no one would notice.

"But would you really want to live here?" I asked.

Sally shook her head. "No, I wouldn't. I mean, it isn't very real."

There might have been money to make in Las Vegas, but the gambling was a strain and my writing had suffered. I decided that when I finished my degree, I'd pack up my bags and move back to New York.

17 ♠ The Files

I'll always think of the borough of Manhattan as a birth canal. Long, thin, and prone to contractions, it pushed me from its upper half (108th and Broadway, where I stayed my first three months out of school) down through the Village to a tiny one-bedroom in Brooklyn. I'd moved in with a boyfriend whom I'd met back in Iowa, but the two of us had broken up, and I lived there alone before finding a roommate, who slept on the living room couch.

The place had been a steal. It was on the top floor of a three-story building, the other two stories their own separate unit. A filthy, cat-crazed couple and their friend had lived below, and the cats had apparently pissed in every nook, for the stench of their urine would waft up through the floorboards on hot summer days. Though the smell was just awful, it meant the rent was artificially low, and my boyfriend and I, and later my roommate, simply lit stick after stick of ultrafragrant incense in order to smother the stench.

The original landlord of the property was a well-meaning mother of four who lived in a building just a couple of streets down and was too distracted by her several small children to fumigate, which would have raised the market value of the building considerably. This was fine with my boyfriend and me, and I'd happily drop off our rent every month, walking the two or three blocks to the landlady's house, peering into the kitchen, which was always cluttered with the remnants of some wholesome domestic project or other.

Just after my boyfriend moved out and my roommate moved in, my father had stayed in the place. He was coming to New York to speak to a group of Brooklyn high school English teachers, and I remember he had with him a trench coat that I recognized from when I was young. The two of us had not spoken for a year because of a petty dispute over money, and even though it had been very painful for me, I'd refused to call him. I loved my father, but I couldn't stand to relinquish my position. In poker, they have a way of talking about such matters. They call it "coming over the top," which means, simply, that if someone has raised you, you can assert yourself by reraising them. It's a way of gaining dominance.

I don't remember why or when, but my father and I started speaking again, and he asked if he could stay at my place. Just seeing his face gave me immense pleasure, but I didn't do or say anything. If I had, I might have succumbed in some way—to some fear of his mortality, some wish that I could change the past.

In the morning, we decided to go out to breakfast together,

at one of the several greasy spoons in the neighborhood. We walked a few blocks past the local junior high school. On the sidewalk, a large garbage bag had spilled open. There was a pile of discarded manila envelopes in the gutter. My father needed to send one of his books in the mail and had asked me when he arrived whether I had any envelopes. I didn't, so I'd called a friend and asked him to get some from his office. But here were all these envelopes, crumpled and used, and my father was rifling through them. I started to yell at him to stop. Why did he have to be so cheap? He got angry. He simply didn't understand why such a thing would make me so upset. We started to yell at each other in the middle of the sidewalk. A group of passersby was walking right toward us, so we stopped fighting and went on to breakfast as if nothing had happened.

Later in the day, after my father and I had spent the afternoon walking around the city, catching up on the time that we hadn't been speaking, we went out to dinner at an old Italian restaurant. He ordered the seafood platter, forked a shrimp into his mouth, and held it like a sucker in his lips. He was wearing that trench coat, which brought me back ineluctably to some point in my childhood—when I was nine or ten years old—before my brother left the house for good.

In May of 1998, my Brooklyn idyll came abruptly to an end. A yuppie couple purchased the building and moved into the downstairs apartment. In New York this means only one thing: I was soon to be evicted. I knew that the couple was struggling with their mortgage and when the lease came due, the bickering landlords jacked up my rent by over 50 percent. I was forced to give notice.

As all of this was happening, I was working in the office of a prominent Freudian analyst on the Upper East Side. A charming old man with a mildly stooping posture and a very high hourly rate, he had been voted City's Best Psychoanalyst by a glossy magazine, and though he wasn't my personal therapist, he made me feel safe. Riding on the subway every morning was like an escape from jail. But then at five o'clock or so, I'd have to go back down the line.

In addition to his duties as an analyst to the miserable wealthy, the doctor was an editor of two renowned scholarly journals. Papers would arrive in the office for review and it was my job to prepare them for his comments, which he'd grumble into his Dictaphone machine. Once I finished transcribing his responses, I'd slip copies of the papers into neon orange folders and file them, a task that left my fingers chapped and sore.

I was an excellent filer with extensive experience. The first job I'd ever had had been in the dusty basement of the hospital back in Concord. Their records were a mess, so they'd hired two young girls (the other a skeletal fourteen-year-old who'd shaved half her head) to go through each file and make sure its contents were in order. They'd decided, in other words, to give two young girls access to the medical records of every single person in that little town. Needless to say, by the time the job was over, I was privy to all the gruesome disorders—the breakdowns, the ulcers, the cases of lice—that had afflicted my neighbors through the years.

I'd also had a job working as the personal assistant to the VP of a well-known entertainment firm. He was a gentle if interestingly obsessional man with thirteen assistants. As the thirteenth and newest addition to his staff, I had precisely two responsibilities: to buy three perfect apples every morning (which I'd rinse off thoroughly and leave in a cubby behind his desk) and to keep in touch with publicists to make sure his stars were behaving, which they rarely were. I was expected to work in the office full-time, but there wasn't enough for me to do, and in order to fill the hours I'd file, a task I undertook with an exaggerated earnestness. I purchased a state-of-the-art labeler and typed out little titles for the folders (Warranties—Electronics—Office; The Croup—Pamphlet—1989; Subscriptions—Magazines—Lapsed; Subscriptions—Magazines—Current, etc.). I then put all the files into a rigid order according to their tabs—left to right, left to right, always in tercets, then the next row would start. Everything was so neat and clean that by the time they laid me off (a mere seven months after they'd hired me), every slip of paper in that office had been filed, a fact that my supervisor (yet another assistant) conveyed with immense admiration and respect to the doctor when he called her for a reference.

As I packed up my things, I took solace in the fact that if worse came to worst, I could sleep on the analyst's couch. It was mid to late spring, a little damp, a little cool outside. After waiting through the afternoon to see if some beautiful specter would rescue my poor helpless self, I had ordered three Russians to come by and take my belongings to a storage space on Bond Street. I was certainly despondent (I wept and swept and wept and swept), but I was also elated. I felt free.

But the fact remained: I didn't have money, and I'd avoided admitting this to myself until it was too late at night (and too late in life) to do anything responsible about it. The one thing I could think to do was to call up my brother and ask him for a loan. I was dreading the call, and I spent several hours looking out at the sunset, avoiding, avoiding.

Once I got up my nerve to dial the number, and before I had

to grovel, Howard told me that a friend of his named Landry (they called him Landry the Lock; he was tight with his money) held the lease on a rent-controlled apartment near Gramercy Park. I'd met Landry once or twice. He was short, with a simian face—button nose, vivid eyes—and screwed up. The last time I'd spoken with him, I'd complained of being tired, unable to concentrate, and he'd recommended that I get a prescription for Adderall or, if that wasn't possible, Ritalin.

"I took Ritalin for a long time," he told me. "I used to stay up for three days straight, it was great." My brother said Landry was eager to find a new tenant for his place, and so my eviction was in fact a very happy coincidence.

I received a small white security envelope in the mail two days later. There were keys, but no note. I took a cab to the apartment and stood for a moment on the sidewalk, exultant. The terra-cotta moldings were elegant and well maintained and the flowers on the windowsills burst out from their boxes in thick, luscious coils. I walked through the door, down a dim, narrow hallway, giddy at having a place to live. But when I entered the apartment, I was met with an unfortunate surprise: I was standing in the middle of a bookie office.

I knew it was a bookie office for a number of reasons. There was, first of all, the fact that all the windows had been covered with swatches of industrial gray carpeting. These were affixed to the casements with nails so that it took me all night just to pull a couple off and see the alley. There were also the phones—there must have been ten or so—each one abuzz on a table in the stuffy room. Just to the right of the entrance to the room there was a Fellowes Power Shredder, next to which a bookie had taped a little fortune:

`A gambler will lose not only what he has,`
`but also will lose what he doesn't have.`
`Lucky numbers: 7, 24, 25, 28, 30, 40.`

On the table, next to the phones, a computer glowed a baby blue. One icon especially caught my attention: underneath a cluster of balls—a baseball, a basketball, a football—were the words *The Schedule.* When I clicked on this document, a database appeared (it was blank, its contents presumably hurriedly erased). I went back to the desktop, picked an icon called "Garo" at random, and read:

`Welcome to Action Park!`
`Do you know the secret password?`

I hit Return. "Good afternoon, Mary," the computer said. Then it blinked and went fuzzy and I had to hit 9 to escape. I gave up on the computer, figuring it wasn't my business in the end, and besides, I was feeling really dizzy, not so much because I was frightened by the thought of getting in trouble, but rather because the place was such a mess. After slumping in an office chair and thinking on my options, I rummaged through the filing cabinet drawers, hoping I'd find something helpful, some number to call and complain. Instead I found tapes. Tens, even hundreds, of Maxell cassettes, each with a date: 9/18; 3/24; 5/03. . . . The bookies had apparently recorded their bets in case of some later dispute. I picked up a tape, turned it over in my sullied hands, and carefully replaced it. I didn't think it wise to leave my prints.

The next morning, I woke up to the buzz of my cell phone. It was one of the bookies. A woman with a southern drawl.

"You'll have to trash the tapes," she said. I told her that I'd guessed as much. "But not in the front of the building," she went on. "You take all those tapes and you dispose of them as far away from the building as you can. The FBI—they'll go through the garbage. The police . . . if anyone's casing the place, they'll follow you around, so be careful."

After going out for coffee and walking around, I returned to the apartment and tidied up further. I unplugged the phones (there was a complex contraption at the base of the window from which the wires swiveled menacingly out), put them in boxes, then under the sink. I broke down the tables, shoved them into the closet, and then threw out the chairs. When I finished, I eyeballed the filing cabinet drawers.

I went to the kitchen, pulled a trash bag from its yellow box, then proceeded to stuff it with tapes. When I finished, I tied the bag as tightly as I could, shoved it in another bag, and put the whole mess in a blue vinyl suitcase.

After entering on the uptown side of the Lexington train and walking to the end of the platform, I scanned the vicinity for other riders. There was no one around and as the cars sped through the tunnel, their swoosh blocking out all the racket in my head, I stuffed both the trash bag and the suitcase in the garbage can. Then I boarded the train.

• • •

The room that I worked in at the therapist's office was as tiny as a closet, with a very large window that faced out on a dark alley. In front of the window, there was a miserable sapling, I'm not sure what kind, but it was all I saw of green while I worked in that office. And I'd stare at it for hours. The only item of furniture in the room aside from my desk was an enormous filing cabinet. Beige, with two intimidating drawers, it was the size of a refrigerator laid on its side. There were also two long bracket shelves crammed full of files. Thirty-page papers on all sorts of topics—object relations, schizophrenia, borderline personality disorder—flooded the office, four or more a day, and it took me several hours just to catalog each one and get it ready for the doctor.

When he wasn't editing papers, the doctor held sessions with his patients, and I would use this time to read up on the latest in contemporary psychology. I became a veritable encyclopedia of mental disorders, and, as had happened back in Berkeley, I took quite a few on for myself. I was histrionic, that I knew. I also had a narcissistic, masochistic, borderline personality and hypochondriacal tendencies. Once I finished diagnosing myself, I started in on my friends, then the doctor's own patients. Mrs. Elton over there was clearly a borderline personality disorder. Anyone could see that from the way she smoked her cigarettes. And Mr. Bradshaw, the loudmouthed editor of a well-known New York magazine—why, he wasn't just a narcissist, he also had trouble with his object relations, at least if his treatment of me was anything to go by.

At some point, the papers were no longer even fun to read, but by then I was completely hooked. The room was such a humid little space, and I would pull out a drawer, hoist a pile of neon folders on the floor, then sit on a carpet and tear through the papers as if they were potato chips. My ankles would chafe against the rug and I'd rub them, waiting for the doctor to retrieve whatever patient was waiting outside and leave me to the tears that would inevitably arrive when I'd conclude that it was I who was the patient in the paper.

Whether he knew that I was crying all day long or whether he could somehow just sense that my life had turned sour, the doctor came into my tiny little room one day and asked me to lunch at the Mark Hotel, a very fancy place. I put my hands to my cheeks, which were chapped from my bawling.

"Let me put on some makeup," I said. The doctor told me he didn't see the need, but if I felt I had to, that was OK by him.

In the mirror in the bathroom, I looked a wreck. I filled my palms with cold water and slapped them on my face and neck. When I stepped out of the bathroom, the doctor regarded me strangely. "Everything will be OK," he said. "We'll have a nice time."

After stepping across the street and entering a beautiful lobby, we were seated. The chairs were plush, the other diners, like the doctor, very wealthy and old.

"Order anything you want," he said. "This is your special day."

I turned my face away. "But I haven't done anything," I said. "In fact, I've been very lazy today." What I'd really been doing was sitting in the middle of the humid office weeping, but I didn't put it that way. "I've been a *very* lazy girl."

The doctor smiled. "I think you underestimate yourself." He laughed. "You're an excellent assistant. You really are." I couldn't tell if he knew that I spent all my time sitting reading through the papers. "You get the job done," he continued, looking warmly at my face. "That's the thing that really counts."

When the waiter came over, both of us ordered the Cobb salad, which arrived right away. After eating I felt better, and I thought it a good time to ask for a vacation, which I sorely needed. "I'd like to go to Vegas," I said. "I need to see my brother." The doctor raised an eyebrow.

"Why does your brother live there?"

I told him about my siblings and my mother, that they gambled for a living.

"My mother's gone now," I said. "She moved to Montana with my sister and her little girl. And my brother had to sell his house. His offices were busted."

The doctor nodded. "You know, there's a great literature on the subject of gambling," he said. "I should lend you a book. . . ."

"Really?" I said.

"The traditional line is that gamblers are masochists."

"Masochists?"

"They like to punish themselves, to be punished."

"No, I think you're wrong," I said, shaking my head. "I think my brother and sister are different. They win. They're not losers."

"But *all* gamblers are losers," the doctor said. "Because, in the end, if you gamble, you're playing against fate, and fate always wins. Whatever your brother may win, it sounds like he just had a run-in with the authorities, no?"

I nodded. "But my sister, she's a sadist—definitely a sadist."

"I doubt that she's a sadist," the doctor went on. "You know, I treated this one gambler, an excellent card player. I think he was one of the best in New York. And the thing was, he always found a way to get rid of his money. If it wasn't on the cards, then he'd find something else—women or cars. He was always in debt.

"And I'd say to him, 'Mr. Alwyn, you have to get out of this racket,' and he'd smile and tell me that, yes, he knew. And one day he just stopped coming. I think he went off to law school or something. And I wonder still what happened with his gambling. Did he lose all his money? And the thing was, I knew that even if he stopped with the poker, he would still be a gambler at heart, because even if you stop playing cards, and even if you stop betting horses, there's always something left in life to gamble on."

18 Who Wants to Be a Millionaire?

I took a cab to my mother's hotel. It was nighttime, very warm. She was slated to appear on the then popular TV game show *Who Wants to Be a Millionaire,* and I needed to give her a turquoise rabbit that I'd found in my apartment. Turquoise was her birthstone. The rabbit would bring her good luck.

She was staying in the Empire, a Midtown hotel several blocks from Lincoln Center. She wasn't in her room. I went outside. A show was getting out and the beautiful people in their gently pressed suits were milling about, enjoying the cool evening air. I gamboled around their periphery, searching their faces to see if she might be among them.

When I found her, she was sitting on the crowded patio of an Italian restaurant. I waved. She didn't see me. I jumped up and down on the mica-flecked asphalt. (It looked like snow, snow in the summer, the sidewalk was sparkling.)

"Come here, Kate," she called. "I'm here. Over here." I walked toward the stanchion, unhooked the green velvet rope, and went in.

"Do you want any dinner?" she asked. The game show producers had given her $150 in spending money. "I'm going to spend it *all on food,*" she announced, putting some steak in her mouth. "You can have some if you want."

I told her that I liked what she was wearing, an off-white blouse and pair of charcoal slacks. "I'm not wearing this tomorrow, you know," she said, smiling. "You know, I haven't had my spirits this high for years. I've been reading all these books and learning new things. And Howard's been trying to teach me all about implied odds, but that's going out the window if I get up in the Hot Seat."

"You'll either win the million or you won't," I said. "It's a once-in-a-lifetime sort of thing, not a regular gamble."

"That's right," she said. "I know I've been *so* lucky. I mean, I think I am so lucky to have even gotten here because when I made it to the playoffs I thought, 'Oh, I'll get to see what it's like to play the second level,' because I never in a million years thought I'd make it past that round.

"And you know, just the other day, I was soaking my feet and I couldn't get up and then Oprah came on—because I wouldn't normally watch *Oprah*—and she started talking all about this thing called a gratitude journal, because, you know how she likes to do inspirational stories and things like that."

"Yes, I know."

"Because I wouldn't normally watch *Oprah*. But I think I'm

going to start keeping a gratitude journal because there are so many things I'm grateful for. . . . Did I ever tell you about the most wonderful day of my life? I remember it so well: we were living in the dormitory complex and I was sitting in the kitchen with that burnt-orange carpet and you were very young and the light was streaming in through the windows. I was looking up a word for my puzzle in the encyclopedia, and I kept flipping the pages and I found this one entry, did you know? I found this one entry that said both giraffes and humans have seven vertebrae in their necks, and I just couldn't believe we had the same number.

"And so I think I need to put that in my gratitude journal too," she continued, looking wistfully out at the sidewalk. "That I got a spot on *Millionaire* and that I got to find out that we have just as many vertebrae as giraffes. You know, it was so funny when Oprah told us about hers, because she's been keeping a journal her whole life, since she was fifteen or something, but she decided to try this gratitude journal and it was so funny because she was always writing things like 'Oh, that wonderful bread at the restaurant,' because, you know"—my mother brought her face up close to mine—"because you know how Oprah loves food."

When I was very young and the five of us still lived together, I'd sit with my mother on the green and blue plaid couch while she watched her game shows. She loved them all—*Family Feud, The Price Is Right,* and, especially, *Wheel of Fortune. Wheel of Fortune* was her favorite because it wasn't just about winning money and it wasn't just about trivia, it was also about solving puzzles. I would try very hard, when I sat with my mother, to discover the answer before she did, but I almost never could.

On very rare occasions, usually when the solution had to do with something only a kid would know, like the name of some character on *Sesame Street,* I'd blurt out the answer, get off the couch, and jump up and down. My mother would giggle (she wasn't as competitive as my father), hoist me up in her lap, and tell me I was a very smart girl and that one day I might be as good as she was at word games and puzzles. Though I wasn't exactly sure whether that was my ultimate ambition in life, I welcomed the praise.

So *Millionaire* was just the most recent in a series of family obsessions. When the show came on air, my brother would slump in his armchair in Vegas, my mother would recline in her brown leather lounger, my sister would lie, her legs splayed, on her bed—and the three of them would proceed to commune with the host of the show, Regis Philbin.

When the show broke for commercials, my sister would speed-dial first Mother, then Howard, and lambaste the resident contestant. "What a *moron,*" she'd say. "What do they do when they get people for this show? Ask them if they're *morons*? Is being a *moron* a requirement? Is being a *moron,* like, some sort of prerequisite to being a *total idiot*?" In order to right such wrongs, the three of them would call up every day to try to qualify. There were two qualifying rounds, each of which required immense discipline and patience to pass. There were many afternoons during which my mother or my siblings would be wholly unavailable, waiting for a call from the producers.

One day, based on his estimate of how many people watched the show, how many he figured called in, and how many got on, Howard calculated the odds that he would make it to the Hot Seat. He came to the conclusion that even if he called every day, he still had only the most minuscule chance of appearing. But Howard was clever, and he realized quickly that if he and Mom and Annie banded together, their odds on some part of the million would increase. He asked them to go in for thirds.

By the time Mom arrived in New York for the taping, she'd been practicing Fast Fingers on a cardboard facsimile of the show's device that my sister had constructed. She'd also been playing the computerized version for hours at a time, sitting in her nightie, a lukewarm cup of coffee to her right. Annie and Howard were two of her Lifelines. My father was another, and I was what the people at the game show called her "Special Friend."

"But I still won't know what to say if they ask me a question about pop music," she said as we walked down the sidewalk. We had finished our dinner. She was going to the market to pick up some soda before going to bed. "I mean, Annie's good with middle-brow culture—because you know how she likes her *People*—and Howard knows all about sports and your father knows all about English, but no one knows about pop music. I guess, if I'd made you one of my Lifelines instead of my Special Friend, you could have answered any questions about Duran Duran—oh, do you remember how much you loved them?—but I guess it's too late. . . ." I told her she'd be fine. She nodded her head, took a pull on her Merit.

"I miss New York," she said. "But it's a very expensive city, and I can hardly afford to get a fence in Columbus, let alone a nice apartment here." She sighed. "If I win any money, the first thing I'm going to do is buy a fence so the deer can't get in and eat all the blackberries."

"Right," I said.

"But I can't imagine that I'll win, and even if I do, I'll have to split the money with Howard and Annie. Oh, how I wish I hadn't agreed to that deal now!"

· · ·

Small like a boy, but with a powdered, grown-up face, Regis Philbin, the host of the show, stood at the center of the soundstage. I'd been acutely aware of him for many years, first as the host of *The Regis Philbin Show* and then as the host of *Who Wants to Be a Millionaire,* which, at the time of the taping, was the highest-ranked program on prime-time TV.

When I first arrived at the studio, I'd been impressed. It was housed in a nondescript if posh building, more of a mansion than the site of a soundstage. For just a moment, as I stepped out of the taxi, I could taste the wealth and power in the air, could feel it on my tongue and lips, something savory but sour.

I'd then been ushered into a long line, even though I was the Special Friend and invited guest of one of the contestants. It was as if I were being herded, and I reasoned in defense of this treatment that they must receive at least forty of these Friends a day, all believing they had some special dispensation to traipse right through the double doors to Regis and the soundstage.

I was wearing inappropriate clothing, the ushers told me as they led me to the back. They preferred it when members of the studio audience wore dark clothes, no patterns, no colors. They wanted you to match the set. It was a gelatinous indigo, the ganglionic wires like squiggly veins beneath the stage.

A woman came up to me, my mother's handler, and gave me a pen and a contract. I was signing my life rights away, she told me. I asked her what that meant and she shrugged. "It's really no big deal," she replied, and so I signed.

And then the day grows so slow in my mind, as if time were a flag and no wind. I was watching as my mother and the other nine contestants emerged and sat down in the chairs that encircled the Hot Seat. Regis was sitting in the center of the stage. He was waiting for the champion.

She was small, very blond. She'd slept badly, I think. On a screen, which hung down from the rafters, I could make out her face, the pale skin, the bent nose. Her lips were quivering. She was determined, she said, to win the million-dollar prize.

I looked over at my mother, who was patiently sitting, waiting for her turn to play the game. She was wearing a very pink shirt and a blazer. Her cropped salt-and-pepper hair had been spiked by the stylist backstage. She looked happy, and I thought of all those years she had spent hunching over the table in the kitchen in the dark. She had always loved puzzles, had always loved games, and now she was waiting for her chance to sit down in the middle of the stage in front of everyone and try to win some money.

There is no need to belabor the banal and disappointing events that followed. The shivering blonde, who refused to admit that she didn't know the answer to a question about presidents, sat in the Hot Seat for nearly an hour. She'd run out of Lifelines, and she couldn't remember the presidential order, but the audience had grown hostile, so she guessed and got it right.

The next question Regis posed regarded the U.N. If she answered it correctly, she would win half a million dollars. If not, she would lose nearly all of the money. She sat there again, for a very long time, and shook. She was taking all my mother's time, and my mother wouldn't have another chance. Finally, after a full thirty minutes, she answered the question.

"Is that your final answer?" asked Regis.

"Yes, it is," said the woman.

"Are you sure?"

"Yes, I'm sure."

Regis cleared his throat and announced that the woman was wrong.

In response, the woman threw a fit. She got up off the Hot Seat and balked. Some handlers then appeared and pushed her across the soundstage. Her husband, an accountant who'd been watching from the bleachers, had tried to embrace her, but she'd pushed him away.

After a pause while the audience processed what had happened, two rounds of Fast Fingers were played. One question regarded the board game Monopoly, the other the dreaded category: pop music. My mother got both of them wrong.

When the show finally aired on July 30, they'd cut it down to size. It didn't look like the woman had done what she did. To the audience, all 40 million of them, she appeared not only normal, but pitiable, she'd lost so much money.

This thought made me angry. Not because my mother lost and the woman had taken so much time. What really made me angry was that no one would know the messy truth of the matter.

We all like to think that things work out, to pretend to our neighbors that they make perfect sense. I know my mother does. She spent the rest of the afternoon trying to reason it through, in her boxy little room on the ninth floor of the Empire, calculating and recalculating her odds, thinking about the next time she'd get on the show, and the next time after that. Because she wanted to come back. And I told her that she would come back, even though I knew it wasn't probable.

epilogue

"The Dancing Waters"

I am sitting with Howard in his kitchen in Las Vegas. We are laughing. It is winter, when the air grows thin and the cloud cover comes. Short, cool days, and at night, there is only the game. I drop a glass on the floor. It smashes.

"What a mess," I say.

"It's entropy," my brother says.

Entropy: the theory that the universe tends toward disorder, that everything ordered is destined to fall into savage disrepair.

I disagree. I don't see why a broken glass is any less ordered than a glass full of water.

"What's the difference?" I say. "It's only the human mind that believes in stupid order."

"That's not true," Howard says, opening the microwave. "Order is a very important concept. Order is warm."

"Warm?"

"There's only so much matter in the world," he says. "And when you calculate it, there's an average distance between objects in the universe. When objects come together in a greater than average way—when things like planets and stars and cosmic dust are arranged in a greater than average proximity, then things get warmer."

"So order is when things come together in 'a more than average way' and get warm?" I ask.

"Yes, that's right. It's a very important concept."

"So why wouldn't everything be cold then? Why would anything or anyone come together in a 'more than average way'?"

"Well, that's one of the great mysteries, isn't it?"

Later that night, my brother needs to play. Steve Wynn has recently opened the newest of his luxury casinos. In homage to its theme—Italian, romantic—he has called it the Bellagio and decked it out in Old World style.

I decide to accompany my brother to the place, for I'm eager to see it—and eager to watch him play. He's been winning a lot, has a new, lavish house, a new life.

When we get to the casino, I sit behind Howard, eat a small cut of salmon and some fries. I feel full, so I decide to take a walk.

"I'll see you," I say, leaving Howard to play.

"Yeah, later."

I head out to the front of the casino to watch its new show. I call it "The Dancing Waters," but I'm not sure that's the official name. Outside the casino, on an acre-long tract of land that flanks the Strip, there's a very large lagoon. At night, when the lights come up from underneath the water, and the cars zoom by with their headlights on, and the pedestrians flood over the footbridge from Caesar's or Bally's or the Barbary Coast, the water starts to dance. There's a musical accompaniment, different all the time: Copland, Elvis, Sinatra. And the water shoots up, each long strand of it frothing, synchronically flaring and waving.

The people at the balustrade watch, entranced. It is winter, so they are wearing jeans and sweaters, looking on at the water and listening to the music. The children are fooling around, making a lot of noise. They don't yet understand why this is beautiful and serious; that this is beautiful order, here, in the desert, where, without water, the manicured flowers would grow wispy in the blazing noonday sun.

But the grown-ups know, and I know, because we know about disorder and so we've come here to forget all about it; we stand at this perfect stone balustrade, artfully designed to resemble those of Italy, and are glad for the absence of everything cold and dirty and worn.

When the show is over, we walk up the incline toward the casino, then through the bright, golden doors. We walk by Tiffany's, Armani, and Chanel. We're going toward the machines, which are beautiful and new, like everything here. And we put our money in, because that is what it takes: lots and lots of money. To keep us warm and tidy and clean. To keep us happy.

about the author

Katy Lederer is the author of a poetry collection, *Winter Sex.* A past resident of Berkeley, Las Vegas, and Iowa City, she currently lives in New York City, where she works for a proprietary trading firm.